P9-DYE-325

The ART of ACHIEVEMENT

The secret of life is in art.
Oscar Wilde (1854–1900)

OTHER BOOKS BY TOM MORRIS

Making Sense of It All

God and the Philosophers

True Success

If Aristotle Ran General Motors

Philosophy for Dummies®

The ART of ACHIEVEMENT

Mastering The 7 Cs of Success in Business and Life

Tom Morris

Andrews McMeel Publishing

Kansas City

The Art of Achievement: Mastering The 7 Cs of Success in Business and Life, copyright © 2002 by Tom Morris. All rights reserved. Printed in the United States of America. No part of this book may be used or reproduced in any manner whatsoever without the written permission except in the case of reprints in the context of reviews. For information, write Andrews McMeel Publishing, LLC, an Andrews McMeel Universal company, 4520 Main Street, Kansas City, Missouri 64111.

07 08 09 RDH 10 9 8

Library of Congress Cataloging-in-Publication Data

Morris, Thomas V.
The art of achievement : mastering the 7 Cs of success in business and life / Tom Morris.
p. cm.
ISBN-13: 978-0-7407-2201-1
ISBN-10: 0-7407-2201-8
1. Success—Psychological aspects. I. Title.

BF637.S8 M67 2002
158.1—dc21 2001053267

Book design by Lisa Martin

ATTENTION: SCHOOLS AND BUSINESSES

Andrews McMeel books are available at quantity discounts with bulk purchase for educational, business or sales promotional use. For information, please write to: Special Sales Department, Andrews McMeel Publishing, LLC, 4520 Main Street, Kansas City, Missouri 64111.

TO MARY

For your encouragement,

straight talk,

and cute shoes

CONTENTS

PREFACE

This book is about the ancient art of achievement. It's about making good things happen in business and in life. It's also a book of philosophy such as you may never have seen before. It will lay out some of the most practical and powerful guidance for living ever articulated by the world's great thinkers. It's all about growth, excellence, and the experience of a deep satisfaction in everything we do. It's ultimately about making our mark in this world by mastering some of the most effective tools that have ever been devised for creative and fulfilling achievement.

The greatest philosophers of the past have left us a huge bank account of wisdom for successful living, but most people don't even know it exists. We are the proper inheritors of these great thinkers, but we tend to approach life with just our own resources and whatever insights we can pick up from the people around us. We need more. As a contemporary philosopher, I've discovered this ancient wealth of wisdom, and I've seen the difference it can make for anyone's life. In these pages I want to share some of it with you.

SEVEN CONDITIONS AND SEVEN ARTS

For at least the past twenty-five hundred years, the best diagnosticians of the human condition have given us insights about seven universal conditions of success that must be used if we want to put ourselves into the best possible position to accomplish our dreams. Associated with each condition is an art. This book is about mastering those seven conditions and seven arts.

We're all capable of becoming artists in nearly everything we do. This is an essential realization for experiencing the sort of personal growth and lifelong adventure that is most productive of innovative, long-term success. Satisfying achievement is always an artistic accomplishment.

By artist I mean of course everyone who has tried
to create something which was not here before him,
with no other tools and material than the
uncommerciable ones of the human spirit.
William Faulkner (1897–1962)

I should make clear how I'm using the concept of art. To be an artist, you don't have to hold a brush, bend metal, chisel rock, or play a musical instrument. Any creation of human skill is a work of art. Creating a great business, or a great career, is art. Developing your own talents, or cultivating a wonderful family life, is an art. Art transforms what is. It's the creative impulse in every human heart. The nature of our success will depend on the artistry of our actions day to day.

The ancient philosopher Aristotle (384–322 B.C.) had his own take on this. In his characteristically convoluted way he said:

> The business of every art is to bring something into existence, and the practice of an art involves the study of how to bring into existence anything that is capable of having such an existence and has its efficient cause in the maker and not in itself.

To put it simply, our success in life ultimately will depend on what we know, what we do, and what we become as a result. As Aristotle saw, we can't reasonably expect to attain the highest and most significant forms of success without studying and mastering the art of achievement.

Art is not a thing: it is a way.
Elbert Hubbard (1856–1915)

THE REAL SECRET OF SUCCESS

There are no scientific laws or magical formulas for success. Publishers can't figure out what produces a bestseller. Toymakers can't predict the next fad. Some well thought out ventures succeed and others that seem just as promising don't.

Fortune may smile on you today and pull the rug out from under you tomorrow. Human beings have free will, and the responses of other people to what we do can never be completely assured. The individuals we most want to reach may embrace our projects or not, despite all our best efforts.

People have always searched for some form of achievement alchemy—a ritual to practice, an incantation to perform, a series of actions that will guarantee the exact form of success they seek. Many "secrets" have been proclaimed, but not one has proved to be as reliable as promised.

Superstition, which is widespread among the nations, has taken advantage of human weakness to cast its spell over the mind of almost every man.

Cicero (106–43 B.C.)

There is no technology of success, and there is nothing weirdly mystical about it, either. No magic talismans or voodoo incantations can alter the realities we face in the world. No simple formulas can force the hand of fortune. Real achievement doesn't happen that way. It's not a matter of science or magic. But it is a matter of art. This is the real secret of success. There is a performance art to achievement. In fact, there are several.

Henry Wadsworth Longfellow believed that "Art is power." And I agree. In this book, we'll look at the forms of art that can empower us to live more successfully, more fully, and more meaningfully, in our work as well as in the more private spheres of our personal experience.

NO ONE IS STUCK

Not long ago, when I was checking in to a Florida hotel, a bellman walked up and asked whether I had ever taught at Notre Dame. I replied yes, I had for many years. He said, "Notre Dame is in Indiana, right?" I told him it is, in South Bend. "Well," he said, "there was a guy from Indiana here a few weeks ago. He had been a farmer all his life, and had never traveled. The farm went bust and he ended up as a salesman. He came here on his first sales conference. The first plane ride of his life, the first hotel visit. Amazing. He arrived with his boss, they checked in, and his boss told him to go upstairs, put his bags in the room, and meet him back in the lobby in five minutes. He went up. Ten minutes passed. Fifteen minutes. Maybe twenty. Finally the boss grabs a house phone, calls up, and says, "Hey, what's going on? It's been twenty minutes and we've got a session to get to!" The fellow from Indiana said, "I'm stuck and I don't know what to do. I'm in my room and there are only three doors. One's a bathroom, one's a closet, and the other one has a sign on it that says, 'Do Not Disturb'!"

He who is not aware of his ignorance will only be misled by his knowledge.

Richard Whately (1787–1863)

I laughed and thanked the bellman for his entertaining tale, and I reflected for a moment on what it showed. The philosophical moral is simple. Sometimes we need help to read the signs of the times, and the signposts of our lives. Too many people in our day feel either stuck, or confused, or both. There are doors of opportunity all around, options for the taking, but we often don't know which of these will lead to where we really want to go.

The great philosophers can help point the way. They can guide us with insights we can use to grow and then flourish. They can position us to think in new ways about our lives and empower us to open doors of personal and professional success that might otherwise remain closed. No one is really stuck in life. We just need wise advisers to show us the way forward.

Know your opportunity.

Pittacus (ca. 650–ca. 570 B.C.)

INTRODUCTION

From ancient times to the present day, across all cultures and throughout the centuries, wise people who have thought deeply about success and excellence have left us bits and pieces of advice for attaining the right kind of achievement in our lives. I've put all these insights together into a simple, comprehensive, and logically connected framework of seven universal conditions for achieving satisfying and sustainable results in any endeavor. I call them "The 7 Cs of Success."

The 7 Cs of Success

1. A clear **Conception** of what we want, a vivid vision, a goal clearly imagined.
2. A strong **Confidence** that we can attain our goal.
3. A focused **Concentration** on what it takes to reach that goal.
4. A stubborn **Consistency** in pursuing our vision.
5. An emotional **Commitment** to the importance of what we're doing.
6. A good **Character** to guide us and keep us on a proper course.
7. A **Capacity to Enjoy** the process along the way.

Together these make up a universal tool kit for remarkable accomplishment. They constitute the most extraordinary leveraging device for our energies in any situation or challenge. Nevertheless, though they are incredibly powerful, they are not magic. They won't turn couch potatoes into decathlon champions overnight. They can't guarantee anyone a million dollars, world fame, or the presidency. But they are remarkably reliable tools for helping us make the most of our lives and energies every day.

Give us the tools and we will finish the job.
Winston Churchill (1874–1965)

These seven simple conditions of success are a bit like the oils and brushes of a painter, or the hammers and chisels of a sculptor. They are the tools of a distinctive art form: the art of achievement. And there is an art to applying each of them in our lives.

SEVEN? WHY SEVEN?

You may find yourself asking, "Why exactly seven conditions and arts, rather than five, or nineteen, or thirty?" What's so special about the number seven, anyway? We're told by Stephen Covey that there are *Seven Habits of Highly Effective People*. Depak Chopra writes *The Seven Spiritual Laws of Success*. Another author follows up with *The Seven Spiritual Secrets of Success*.

And then of course there are the original seven seas, the Seven Wonders of the World, seven continents on earth, *The Seven Samurai,* seven sages of the ancient world, the seven hills of Rome, *The House of Seven Gables,* seven days in the week, the seven nutritional food groups, seven fat years and seven lean years, the Seven Sisters, Seventh Heaven, *The Seventh Seal,* the seven dwarfs, *Seven Brides for Seven Brothers,* the seven-year itch, *The Magnificent Seven,* and that ever-refreshing soft drink, 7-Up.

What gives? Are we on to something weird and mystical here? I'm afraid the answer is: No. But we are on to something surprisingly useful, which is one reason local telephone numbers for quite some time have had no more than seven digits. Many psychologists suggest that the largest grouping the human memory can naturally handle well is a group of seven. Let's see—Sleepy, Dopey, Doc, Droopy? Grouchy?—I guess it's a good thing there aren't four hundred, or even twenty-three, universal conditions for success. Seven of anything is hard enough to recall.

There are three things I always forget.
Names, faces, and—the third I can't remember.
Ettore Schmitz (1861–1928)

There was no contrivance on my part to make it come out this way. I wasn't looking for exactly seven conditions. I simply cast my net as widely as I could, searching the writings of all the great thinkers, analyzing the stories of truly successful people, and interpreting my own experience. The 7 Cs just emerged. Now they have been road-tested for many years in work with accomplished individuals from every walk of life. I've come to believe that any other facilitator of success that we might think of is just the practical application of one of these conditions to a specific challenge, and in that way ends up being further confirmation of the complete comprehensiveness of this framework of seven.

I'm sure you'll find, as you think about each of these conditions, that you have been acting in accordance with at least some of them already to achieve the good you've already attained in your life. But now you'll be able to come to a greater awareness and understanding of each of them, as well as of how they're related to each other in an overall framework for satisfying success. I'm hoping that you will be able to test the whole framework in your life and that as a result you will come to experience the great power of this tool kit for achievement in everything you do.

THE POWER OF THE 7 CS

It has often been said in recent years that success is not a destination, but a journey. The same could be said about each of the seven conditions for achievement. We never attain any of them once and for all. They are creative, progressive, skill-based, and directional matters of attitude and behavior. In this book, we will examine each of these seven conditions and each of their associated arts in a way that will let you see vividly how they apply in your own life right now. With their help, you'll also be able to discern how the other people around you can better realize their potential excellence. You'll be able to spot trouble, diagnose problems, find solutions, and initiate productive change like never before. We have here a potent form of practical art based on the very deepest truths about attainment and human nature.

Art is not a mirror held up to reality,
but a hammer with which to shape it.
Bertolt Brecht (1898–1956)

The 7 Cs and their related arts can move you farther along the road to accomplishing any good thing you desire. You can use them to pursue more effectively whatever you want in life. But the first question is, of course, what do you want? And then: Is this really right for you, given your talents, experiences, relationships, commitments, likes, and dislikes? It's one thing to attain success in the pursuit of any given goal, another altogether to choose successfully the goals that are best for you to pursue.

Do you need to increase your financial resources? Or do you want to put them to a better, nobler use? Would you like to be more widely known for what you do? Or would you enjoy exercising your talents on a broader scale? Have you ever aspired to leave a legacy beyond your work? Would you like to make a bigger difference for good in the lives of the people around you?

How about your relationships? How's your family life? Could it be better than it is? If you're married, is that marriage growing, or is it gradually breaking down? If you have children, do you feel a great satisfaction in actively parenting them, or are they nearly strangers to you? What about close friendships? Are you experiencing any growth on that front, or is everything stagnant?

Think for a moment about your spiritual life. Do you give enough time to yourself to cultivate and enjoy the finer things of the spirit? Do you feel any sort of deep connection with something greater than the self? Do you ever sense that you are on any sort of a mission in life, or are you disconnected from deeper sources of meaning? Could this side of your life use some improvement?

The man who has no inner life
is the slave to his surroundings.
Henri Frédéric Amiel (1821–1881)

How about the physical you? How's it going there? Are you rested? Do you eat right and get enough sleep? Is your body as active as it needs to be? Are you discovering new physical talents, or at least still developing old skills? Do you enjoy exercise on a regular basis with family or friends?

How do you feel about your overall contribution to the larger community around you? Do you do enough for others, sharing the best of who you are, what you know, and what you have? Or could this area stand some improvement?

What is the use of running
when we are on the wrong road?
Bavarian Proverb

With the help of The 7 Cs of Success and their companion arts, you can launch into new adventures, create new relationships, improve old ones, work more efficiently, accomplish more, attain greater health in the outer and inner person, and find deeper satisfaction in what you do. If your life and energies are scattered all over the place, you can also use The 7 Cs to do less and feel better about it, enjoying the greater results that ensue from properly targeted living. Nobody else knows exactly what's right for you and how you should apply these universal conditions for success to attain your own form of personal excellence. Only you can decide.

TRUE SUCCESS

Before we explore some very practical issues about the means of attaining success in any particular enterprise, we need to reflect for a bit on the question of what success in life really and most fundamentally is. Too many people seem to be chasing the wrong things. Getting equipped to go faster down the wrong road has never been a recipe for human happiness. How we think about success can make a huge difference in how we experience life.

> *The impression forces itself upon one that men measure by false standards, that everyone seeks power, success, riches for himself, and admires others who attain them, while undervaluing the truly precious things in life.*
>
> Sigmund Freud (1856–1939)

When my father lay dying of lung and brain cancer in a hospital room in Durham, North Carolina, my mother and I sat vigil by his bed. After a long period of silence one day, she said to me, "You know, your dad never really felt like a success." I was shocked. I had always thought of him as a tremendous success in every way.

Growing up on a farm, Hugh Thomas Morris had developed every skill little boys admired. He made beautiful slingshots from the small crooks of dogwood-tree branches, and his marksmanship with them was astonishing. He could throw a can into the air and hit it on the first try. He once shot a lizard off a friend's shoulder. I even saw him once place a wooden match upright in a crack in a picnic table, walk off several paces, turn, and light the match with his third shot.

This was a man who could build a snow fort like something in a movie. He designed and created model rockets that awed my whole school. He invented and built toys all the time—a rubber-band rifle, a skate scooter, a rolling hoop device of the kind that kids had played with in the 1920s, and big kites made from newspaper and reeds that would disappear like pin dots into the sky. He hammered together jumping boards, a wooden apparatus a lot like a foot-high seesaw that we'd use standing up. I'd perch on one end and then another kid would jump on the opposite tip, shooting me into the air. Landing, I would launch my friend, and so on, until somebody crashed. We had never heard of legal liability.

The great man is he who does not lose his child's heart.
Mencius (ca. 371–ca. 291 B.C.)

My dad built a clubhouse for me and my friends that was the envy of the neighborhood. Every kid around could fit into it. He even installed an old radio in there that could pick up China. At least, that's what we thought when we turned the big dial to a scratchy station in a foreign language. He had taught us how to stretch radio wire across the yard, back and forth, to make a huge antenna. We wouldn't have been surprised to be the first to hear aliens invading the earth.

H. Tom Morris would take us on hikes, through the woods and along the banks of beautiful creeks, that were as exciting as any adventure to the Andes or Himalayas. Half a day could be spent exploring territory where we were sure no human being had ever been. I'm surprised I never came across a *National Geographic* reporter or photographer. Our team of neighborhood wanderers would have made a fine focus for a feature story. And this was all a few minutes' walk from my house, at the edge of the city limits, where Durham, North Carolina, met the Great Unknown.

The leader of the pack, my dad, was an amateur champion horseshoe thrower and a consistently good badminton player. He grew sunflowers so high we worried about low-flying planes, and he was always quick with a joke.

Let each man exercise the art he knows.
Aristophanes (ca. 448–ca. 388 B.C.)

Not to mention the artwork, the go-carts, the skate scooters, the BB guns, the fishing poles, and how he broke his leg trying the new high jump he had built in the backyard. The wooden swing set he designed for the grandchildren twenty years ago stands to this day. And he did all this while managing a radio station, broadcasting for the Durham Bulls, starting an advertising agency, inventing, manufacturing, and learning the real estate business. How could he not feel like a tremendous success?

With his farm values, he lived modestly. Apart from a rare extravagance, and even that on a small scale, he did not ever seek to live the lifestyle of the rich and famous. He did not soar on the wings of what our society too often holds out as the one and only standard for success: wealth. All I want to say is, "Good for him." So far as I could see, he lived in a way that was good for others, and deeply good for him. He lived his real adventure. And that is true success.

Too many people in our day are tyrannized by false standards and artificial expectations. They feel like failures or also-rans when they are really great successes. By the same token there are people who feel like conquerors when they have sacrificed everything that really matters on the alters of celebrity, wealth, and power.

The achievements that society rewards are won at the cost of diminution of personality.
Carl Jung (1875–1961)

BALANCE

Many people secretly wonder whether success is even possible in our time without any diminution of what really matters. I am convinced that it is, if we refuse to be bullied by artificial standards. But we have to understand the nature of true success first. It requires a measure of balance in what we seek to achieve.

Ask of the gods nothing excessive.
Aeschylus (ca. 525–ca. 456 B.C.)

As a world society, we seem fixated on versions of accomplishment that rely on a nearly freak-of-nature level of talent, monomaniacal focus, and single-minded pursuit. The philosophy of "More" dominates our imaginations—more, bigger, faster, higher, better. The medal-winning Olympic athlete or the dominating professional sports star is our paradigm—people whose childhoods have been sacrificed to relentless training; their relationships stretched or broken by grueling hours of intense practice; their lives led in one dimension, producing an intense burst of world fame. The basketball hero grows up living in the gym, shooting hoops day and night. The rock virtuoso plays his guitar fourteen hours a day, every day of the week. Of course, not all rock and jock stars live unbalanced lives, but many who gain the most attention are exemplars of extremism and life imbalance.

How do the rest of us respond to this model of success? We work from early morning until late at night; we live in airports and hotels, and when we're home, we carry our work with us, in a relentless effort to get the edge and wow the crowds. We sparkle, we flame, and we burn ourselves out, while often alienating the people we love the most and burning bridges we can never rebuild.

The world will always contain a few tortured geniuses and hyperproductive maniacs. But they can't be our sole paradigm for human achievement and personal excellence. That would be a model devoid of any appreciation for the importance of balance in a healthy, sustainable form of life.

Some people worry that balance always comes at the cost of mediocrity. I disagree. True success differs in its contours for different people, but a balance, or harmony, among the various domains of life—between the inner and the outer, as well as the personal and professional—is attainable in some form by everyone. We should never be bullied by the version of extreme, one-dimensional short-burst success celebrated in the media. Rather, each of us should seek to find the balance that's right for us as individuals.

The shoe that fits one person pinches another;
there is no recipe for living that suits all cases.

Carl Jung

Let's think for a moment about balance. Consider the case of high-wire artists. If you've ever seen a close-up of the feet of these performers on television, you may have noticed something interesting. They don't manage a perfectly static balance, walking smoothly along the wire as if it were solid ground. They shimmy a little to the left and then correct to the right, out of balance to one side and then compensating on the other. In real life, this is what maintaining balance requires.

There are no perfectly straight lines in the world, and no completely flat surfaces. These are geometrical abstractions. There's no such thing as a perfect life balance, either. That's just as much an abstraction. Real-life balance is dynamic. It's often shaky, involving lots of movements off to one side and then to the other. It's sometimes smoother, requiring fewer or smaller corrections. But it's those little adjustments that are crucial. The right balance will differ for different people.

Another point is equally important. What the right balance is for you may differ significantly at various stages in your life. What's right in college won't usually work for the middle-aged manager. What's best for the young mother may be very different from what the empty-nester needs. The life balance that works for the young salesman will not likely be right for the senior executive. Life has many stages, and we find ourselves in different adventures along the way. An inability to discern the relevance of these differences for issues of balance can result in problems. We should always understand success with the issue of life balance in mind.

THE SHAPES OF SUCCESS

Albert Einstein (1879–1955) once said, "Possessions, outward success, publicity, luxury—to me these have always been contemptible. I assume that an unassuming manner of life is best for everyone, best for both the body and the mind." I've come to believe that Einstein's judgment on this issue is just as big a mistake as the one made by a person who thinks that money, fame, luxury, and power are the only measures of success. In fact, these two mistakes are like two sides of the same coin. They both derive from thinking that external matters, like money and fame, have just one value in human life, positive or negative, and that they are always decisive.

Money is a good servant, but a bad master.

Francis Bacon (1561–1626)

The best definition of success is simple. True success involves discovering your talents, developing those talents, and deploying them in the world for the good of others as well as yourself through the setting, pursuing, and attaining of appropriate goals. Different people have different talents, different skills, different experiences, and different dispositions. We should also expect to have interestingly different forms of success.

Success in life has many shapes. It need not take the form of extraordinary material wealth or extensive public fame. But neither are these things contemptible. Some people's talents may take them down a road paved with gold because of what their culture happens to value and what other people around them want. There is nothing inherently suspect about the results.

I find all this money a considerable burden.
J. Paul Getty (1892–1976)

For some of us, wealth is a blessing. For others, it is a curse. And the same goes for fame, power, and social status. They are not infallible indicators of true success, by which I always mean deeply satisfying, sustainable, and meaningful achievement in a person's life. But neither are they awful things to be avoided at all costs. We should not all chase them. And we shouldn't all shun them. What matters most is how they relate to the inner person and how they are used.

It's the first of all problems for a man to find out
what kind of work he is to do in this universe.
Thomas Carlyle (1795–1881)

What are you here to do? What am I here to contribute? What do we need for doing our jobs to the best of our abilities, and what will result from doing them well? A great deal of money and fame? This can be good, if it's right for you or me. Very little money and fame? This can be fine, too, depending on what we are here to accomplish and how we are meant to achieve it.

I have become increasingly convinced that, whatever our talents and calling, we are in this world for an adventure of personal growth and positive contribution. We are meant to be exploring, learning, testing ourselves, creating, and discovering new ways to make a difference for others. True success requires an ongoing adventure of self-discovery and art in balanced pursuit of the things that are right for us as the people we are.

How then do we set goals that are right for us? What indeed are the proper objectives that should guide and govern our paths through life? There is an ancient art of goal setting that centers on having a clear conception of what we want. And this is the topic of Part 1.

PART 1

THE ART OF CONCEPTION

Nature scarcely ever gives us the best;
for that we must have recourse to art.

Balthasar Gracian (1601–1658)

CHAPTER

Taking Aim: Targeted Living 1

CONDITION 1 OF THE 7 CS:

*We need a clear **Conception** of what we want, a vivid vision, a goal clearly imagined.*

HAVING GOALS

Aristotle has taught me we all need a target to shoot at. We must have goals to guide our actions and energies. The Greek word for target was *telos.* Human beings are teleological creatures. We are hard-wired to live purposively, to have direction. Without a target to shoot at, our lives are literally aimless. Without something productive to do, without positive goals and a purpose, a human being languishes. And then one of two things happens. Aimlessness begins to shut a person down in spiritual lethargy and emptiness, or the individual lashes out and turns to destructive goals just to make something happen.

The soul that has no established aim loses itself.
Michael de Montaigne (1533–1592)

Most of us have had goals set for us from our earliest years. Our parents gave us instructions; then our teachers did; and finally so did our employers. It's perfectly natural to receive goals from other people. A society can't exist without the sort of cooperative ventures between people that often require one's passing on goals to another. All training, education, and leadership involves setting goals for others to pursue.

But even within that structure, when we have overall work targets given to us, we need to be active ourselves and engage creatively in personal goal setting to move us in the direction of those externally established targets, and to augment what we've been asked to do. No other person knows all our talents, experience, and desires. No one else can possibly guess everything we are capable of contributing. It's up to us to take the initiative, exercise our creativity, and put our personal resources into action in such a way as to add positive value to whatever we're involved in, to delight the other people around us, and to satisfy ourselves as well.

There are aspects of our lives where no one else can establish goals for us. It's up to us what we do with our time and energy. If we waste the opportunity to structure our lives creatively within this realm of freedom, we'll never experience the happiness available to us.

Purpose is what gives life a meaning.
C. H. Parkhurst (1842–1933)

I don't mean to imply that everyone should carry around a planner with each fifteen-minute period of the day structured around goals. That might be fine for some personality types, but for most of us it would amount to replacing our humanity with a page out of a robotics manual. We don't need to burden ourselves with too much structure. An afternoon on the sofa, a day at the beach, or a week relaxing in the mountains can be exactly what you need. I'm just pointing out that, as the ancient Greeks realized, we can do more with our lives, for our world, and for ourselves than we think if we creatively use the time and energy we've been given in pursuit of positive goals that are our own.

THE DILEMMA OF GOAL SETTING

There is one apparently paradoxical feature of goal setting. But behind it is a positive insight. Here's the paradox. Goal setting can appear to bind you to static commitments in a world that's quite dynamic. Suppose you set yourself a goal that looks reasonable today. How do you know that tomorrow it will still make sense? How can you be sure that in the process of pursuing it, you won't see something else that you'd rather accomplish instead? You may come to regret the exclusivity of attention that establishing and pursuing your goal required. You may find yourself moving down a road you end up not liking at all. In a world of flux, it initially seems that we need the structure imposed by goal setting, but it's perhaps this very flux that renders such an activity inappropriate.

I'm all mixed up and I can't keep up
with everything that's happening.
Elvis Presley (1935–1977)

The problem is that when you are moving in the direction of a goal, you always begin to see things you otherwise would not have been positioned to notice, things that you could not have been aware of when deciding which goals to pursue. But these new perspectives may help you see, among other things, that you have set yourself the wrong target. This paradox goes back to a simple fact: Except in the case of fairly trivial goals, we can never know enough at the time of initial goal setting to be sure we have indeed set for ourselves the right goal, one that we'll want to stick with, and one that is truly appropriate for us. In a culture already shy about making commitments, this little insight can be very troubling.

Some people recommend that we not set goals at all, but rather just go with the flow as we drift through life, and concentrate on merely enjoying the ride. Their view often seems to be that goals stultify and cut us off from all the richness that life might otherwise have to offer if we were just more open.

So far as a man thinks, he is free.
Ralph Waldo Emerson (1803–1882)

Goal setting is not a science. But it is an art. It can be a dynamic activity that's extremely flexible and adaptive. When we set goals, we don't chain ourselves down. Our chosen objectives aren't carved in stone. They just give us direction as we move into the future. We set goals the best we can, with the information we have, and then find that as we work toward them, we gather more information that either helps us refine them or else leads us to better goals instead.

A former student had always wanted to be a country music star. So she set some personal goals and moved to Nashville. She was a good singer, but not great. It took little time for her to realize she was just not talented enough to attain her childhood dreams. But in the course of pursuing the goal of vocal stardom, she had met a lot of musicians and people behind the scenes of the music industry. Among other things, she had never before known there was such a job as that of a music business attorney. The more she learned about the business, the more she came to realize the important role a talented lawyer can play in the lives of the singers she had so long admired. And the talents of a music business lawyer were qualities she had in bountiful measure. So, with a few years of extra education, this once aspiring singer was busy cutting deals and facilitating careers for some of her favorite performers. She was a part of the world she loved, and was doing something she was very good at. Should we conclude that her initial goal setting in the direction of becoming a recording star was an embarrassing waste of time? Not at all. If she hadn't set those goals and acted on them, she might never have discovered the other vocation that was ideally suited for her. Formulating objectives and taking action on them had brought her into a position for seeing where her future truly lay. That is often an unexpected yet powerful way that goal setting can work in a life.

Life is a series of surprises.
Ralph Waldo Emerson

The main point to notice here is that a great deal of the information out there in the world concerning what we ought to do can't be accessed while we sit still, or even when we just drift with the flow of events that happen to come our way. It's only when we're focused and engaged, structuring our attention and our action, that we put ourselves into the best position to learn what life has to teach us. In fact, the very best way to learn anything is to engage in a ongoing, directed process of healthy goal setting and pursuit.

THE HIGHEST FREEDOM

Does the enterprise of goal setting encroach on our freedom? The worry that it does is just based on a misunderstanding of what freedom really is. Freedom from having any goals whatsoever is freedom from having any meaning in your life; it's freedom from success, from happiness, and from the deepest sort of fulfillment a teleological, essentially purposive, being needs.

The only point of "freedom from" is to provide for "freedom to." Freedom should not be thought of fundamentally as a negative concept. Having goals we set for ourselves does not take away any freedom that it's good to have. On the contrary, it is the main sort of activity for the sake of which we are free. A life wholly occupied in "going with the flow" will never give us what we most truly need.

Perfect freedom is reserved for the man who lives by his own work and in that work does what he wants to do.
R. G. Collingwood (1889–1943)

That doesn't mean that it's *never* good to "go with the flow." A measure of this can be part of an intelligent process of dynamic, teleological living. Sometimes we should be loose and noncommittal, adopting a wait-and-see attitude toward how things are developing. We may need to stay open to where a new and unexpected flow of events might be leading. In even the most active life, nonaction is sometimes called for, as we allow our previous efforts to bear fruit, or as we watchfully wait for the next opportunity to leverage our energies well.

The major texts of eastern philosophy have wise advice on the path of patience and the episodic need to wait and just be. We sometimes need to shake loose from an urge to make things happen in order to discover how things ought to happen. We don't always have to be taking charge, planning everything, and forcing all the issues. But we do need to give ourselves the overall guidance and empowering structure of regular goal setting and goal renewal to keep us intelligently on our proper path. There are times when it's difficult, and even premature, to form precise long-term goals. But even in those circumstances, we can and should set goals—goals of watchful waiting, attentive yielding, and educational probing.

In healthy goal setting, we both lead and follow. We take charge in some respects, and respond in others. This is part of the inner art of goal conception, and it is a balance that can propel us toward appropriate achievement in any domain of our lives.

There is nothing in the world really beneficial
that does not lie within the reach of an informed
understanding and a well-directed pursuit.
Edmund Burke (1729–1797)

Thoughtful, balanced teleological living ends up being the highest form of freedom there is.

CHAPTER

2 Finding Proper Goals

Facing any challenge or new opportunity, we need to attain as soon as possible a clear conception of what we want, as a guiding force to marshal our energies and structure our efforts. This is the first of The 7 Cs of Success, and associated with it is the first of our seven related arts, the art of conception, or inner goal setting.

When I say that masterful goal setting requires a clear sense of what we want, I don't mean to imply that we always need to enter a new enterprise with a clear conception of what we want to receive from it as a benefit. We do need a clear idea of what we want to contribute, what we'd like to make happen, and what results we hope to see as a consequence of our efforts. Clarity concerning these things is crucial for launching out well in any new endeavor.

Pursue worthy aims.

Solon (ca. 630–ca. 560 B.C.)

THE JOURNEY OF CLARIFICATION

Goal setting is an art, and its skilled practice takes time. We don't often find ourselves in a position to attain any sort of instant, maximum clarity concerning our goals for the future. It's sometimes a struggle to clarify exactly what we do want, and the process can take longer than we'd like. The sooner we can attain this clarity, though, the better. We live much more effectively in this world when we have a clear conception of where we're going.

We use our time best when we set clear and proper goals and structure our activities around them. Too many people waste their time meandering toward the vaguest of goals, squander their lives chasing the wrong goals, or else just languish in habits that may have ceased relating to any goals at all. We can develop every skill imaginable in our chosen area of work, but still fail to think through what we really ought to pursue. Without clear and proper goals, we cannot attain the success of which we're capable.

Perfection of means and confusion of ends
seem to characterize our age.
Albert Einstein

A clear conception of what we want brings with it several benefits. Vague thoughts can't motivate specific behavior. Clear concepts suggest concrete actions. The more clearly we know what we want, the more obvious it will be what we should do.

Second, it's only when we have in mind exactly where we want to go that we can best recognize and use any resources that may come our way as we move forward. The more precise our aim, the more discriminating we can be in our use of time, energy, and all the other factors that facilitate success in any enterprise.

There is an interesting and important psychological angle here. When I'm really focused on a project and know what I'm after, I see things all around that will help me—magazine articles, books, and other bits of information that otherwise I might not have noticed. When I have a clear goal in mind, I tend to have interesting conversations with people that I would not otherwise have had, and these exchanges often help me along in unexpected ways. I learn more, and more efficiently. By my actions and words, I'm broadcasting into the world my intent, and other like-minded people can pick up on those signals and help in the quest. When I'm not clear on where I'm going, this doesn't happen nearly as much.

When a man does not know what harbor he is sailing for,
no wind is the right wind.
Seneca (ca. 4–65)

The first of The 7 Cs is a clear conception of what we want as the initial stage in any enterprise. All the other conditions of success flow from this. The art of conceiving clear goals is then the first of the seven ancient arts of achievement.

SETTING GOALS WITH SELF-KNOWLEDGE

I was once speaking at a small college on the topic of "true success," and after the talk a group of students wanted some advice. One young man, who seemed a bit agitated, said, "Dr. Morris, I've got a problem. I don't have any goals and I don't know how to get any. What do I do?"

One who desires nothing, hopes for nothing,
and fears nothing cannot be an artist.
Anton Chekhov (1860–1904)

A blank canvas. The famous *tabula rasa.* This generates the original philosopher's question: Can something come out of nothing?

The great modern artist Mondrian once said that the most difficult brush stroke in any painting is the first one. A blank canvas presents infinite possibilities. Where do you start? With that first stroke, the process of elimination begins. What should be chosen and what left behind? How does anyone decide where to start with that work of art which is his life?

I recommended to the student what I often advise. I told him to go to a quiet place and sit down to think with some blank paper and a pen or pencil in hand. A computer will do as well. I suggested he begin making some lists: what he doesn't like about his life right now ("Things to Change"), and what he does like about his life right now ("Things to Preserve"). He might then use some more specific categories, like: what he does and doesn't like about his school experience, and then he could move on to his relationships.

I write to discover what I think.
Daniel Boorstin (b. 1914)

The idea is simple. To be appropriate and powerful, goal setting must always be an exercise in self-knowledge. And to acquire the requisite amount of clear self-knowledge for any new goal-setting enterprise, most of us could benefit from a little reflection, in the form of a personal audit. No one's life is so good it couldn't use improvement. And no one's life is so bad it contains nothing worth preserving.

The same thing is true of any business, department, office, or team. We best discover appropriate targets using a process informed by self-knowledge. "What's right for us, given our strengths and weaknesses?" "What's the best use of our talents and resources?" "What have we learned from our past experience that can shape our new targets now?"

The ancient philosopher Thales (ca. 625–ca. 547 B.C.) was as wealthy as he was wise. Because of this, he was often approached by people seeking his insight and advice about life. In answer to the simple question "What is difficult?" Thales is said to have replied, "To know yourself." In response to the question "What is easy?" he said, "To give other people advice." A wise guy indeed. And in answer to the question "What is pleasant?" the philosopher responded, "True success."

This is a great series of remarks. It's very easy to give other people advice. That's why the world is so full of consultants, self-appointed gurus, and armchair commentators ready to offer their opinions on what the rest of us should be doing, whether we ask or not. Advice is one of the most widely available commodities in our world. But good advice is, ironically, hard to find. Anyone who approached Thales for insight was wise to take his questions to a real expert in human nature. And the philosopher did not disappoint.

Thales was astute with each of his answers. All the ancient thinkers recommended self-knowledge, but he was most likely the first to point out that it may indeed be the hardest thing in life to attain. Yet it is the foundation for the most satisfying achievement in our world—true and sustainable success. That's why meaningful success is such a challenge, in nearly every business and in life. Talented people who lack self-knowledge are living with a great disadvantage. They are without the most basic guidance system for powerful and appropriate goal setting.

Know thyself!

Thales (and many other Greek philosophers)

SELF-KNOWLEDGE AND FUTURE SUCCESS

The future of business, and of work generally, is in many ways unpredictable. But one thing is clear. Every worker in the years to come, whether on the front lines or in the executive suites, will need to think of himself as an independent contractor, a specialized vendor of services with a unique brand known to all. This is the only mind-set that will attract the resources, respect, and opportunities to keep our jobs interesting, our businesses strong, and our careers flourishing. And it's an approach to work that requires a healthy measure of self-knowledge.

The importance of self-knowledge in our most creative endeavors is the reason philosophers like Thales wanted us to understand how difficult it is. Business in the future, with all its creative and entrepreneurial possibilities, will demand much more of this rare commodity than ever before. So will living our own personal adventures. Where the possibilities for personal growth are nearly endless, the challenge of making the right choices is great. So I join Thales and all his ancient colleagues in urging: "Know thyself."

Self-knowledge is the foundation of success because it is the proper starting point for healthy goal setting. And when we have enough self-knowledge to get started, an important process begins. Our pursuit of the goals we embrace yields more self-knowledge, which puts us in an even better position for further goal identification, the pursuit of which brings even more self-knowledge, and so on. We have, as a result, a dynamic journey of increasing knowledge and increasing power, an upward spiral of personal growth. Goal setting itself is an adventure into the unknown, and at its best can be a process of personal conquest, enrichment, and empowerment.

For knowledge, too, is itself a power.

Francis Bacon

I recommend to people who feel they have no goals that they make lists of their likes and dislikes, because I firmly believe that our likes and dislikes, our loves and hates, our attractions and aversions, are often the keys to our talents, signs of what we are here in this world to do. They can also be signs of our deepest values.

Ultimately, no goals are right for us unless they are guided and governed by our deepest values. What is right? What is important? What's worth our time? What should we embrace? Where do we stand? In the future, I believe the most fundamental human values increasingly will be appreciated as the touchstones for all goal setting, in business and in other domains of life. Our deepest values connect up with our deepest loves. And working with love is a key to sustainable success in anything we do.

The best people in any enterprise tend to love what they are doing.

Discovering what we like and dislike about a situation, activity, or relationship can be the first clue for what goals we need to set to make positive improvements. By asking ourselves some simple questions, we become clearer about what we want for the future and what direction we need to take.

Writing seems to help most people accomplish this. Writing of the most personal sort. I didn't recommend that the student with no goals should produce a document to share with other people. I urged him to write for himself because it's an activity that by its very nature tends to discipline our thinking and help us produce clarity where only vagueness has been.

Language is the light of the mind.
John Stuart Mill (1806–1873)

Conversation can also help. Each of us has probably had a conversation with another person where we learned something not from what we heard the other person say, but from what we heard ourselves saying. At its best, talking is a form of thinking. Talking through a situation with coworkers or family members can help us see what goals we might need to pursue, and further talk can help us clarify precisely what we need to do. Whether by writing or speaking, using the clear borders of language helps us to think through and be more precise about what we want in any endeavor. And that is crucial for our sense of direction.

AVOIDING THE WRONG GOALS

I love urging people on to the setting of new goals, and the pursuit of new possibilities. But I never want to encourage anyone to launch into a disaster. Success books in the past century focused on the necessity of setting goals, but said far too little about the vital importance of having only appropriate goals.

Life often involves a juxtaposition of opposites. For adventurous and appropriate goal setting, we need to be both bold and cautious—bold enough to launch out into unknown terrain when we hear the call to go forth, yet cautious enough to resist the siren song of goals that might look good from a distance but would not be right for us to pursue. Avoiding the wrong goals can be as important as embracing the right ones. And this is often difficult to do.

The worst of all deceptions is self-deception.
Socrates (ca. 469–399 B.C.)

One of the strongest forces in human life is the power of self-deception. The wisest among us can at times manage to fool ourselves into thinking that something we know deep down to be wrong is actually perfectly permissible, and even advantageous in the circumstances. Sometimes you can get so excited by the prospect of something new that you become disinclined to listen to that little voice deep within whose whisperings might prompt you to reconsider your course. Whether understood as the voice of conscience, the guidance of God, the protection of a guardian spirit, or the uncanny survival instincts naturally provided by our evolutionary past, this inner sense of warning has been reported since the time of Socrates. The great philosopher himself claimed that whenever he was about to do something wrong, a voice within warned him away from that line of action. Self-deception can prevent us from listening to this voice that Socrates thought so important to heed.

Self-deception operates through selective attention and rationalization. It acts to license behavior that is in some way self-defeating or self-destructive. We can deceive ourselves into believing we ought to pursue something that we know deep down to be wrong. And in that way we can set ourselves up for trouble.

Nothing is as easy as deceiving yourself,
for what you wish you readily believe.
Demosthenes (384–322 B.C.)

Unfortunately, there is no magic philosophical immunization against self-deception. But I can share some warning signs. When considering a possible new goal, or launching into a new line of action, it's best to be on the lookout for a few standard leading indicators that self-deception may play a role in your deliberations.

The rules for detecting the likelihood of self-deception are basically the same as they always have been. Little things do matter. If it looks too good to be true, it probably is. In most other ways, things are rarely what they at first seem. When you're the only one who stands to benefit from a project, no one really stands to benefit. People's feelings matter. Time does fly. No enterprise is worth your energy for external results alone. Money isn't everything.

Whenever you're tempted to think otherwise and flout any of these basic truths, beware of self-deception. Alerted to the possibility you may be misleading yourself, you can be on guard and will less likely be deluded into pursuing a false course that will be damaging in the long run. Self-deception is such a powerful force that we cannot guarantee, even if we do see it in operation, that we'll be able to recognize it as such and overturn its recommendations. But we can be watchful, and, when we understand its pervasiveness, we can be less vulnerable to its depredations.

Everyone will occasionally set wrong goals—not just because of self-deception, because erroneous judgment, false information, and incomplete perspectives can result in our pursuing goals that aren't right for us. The next best thing to avoiding inappropriate goals is to quickly realize when we've gotten on the wrong path and to make a course correction, taking action to veer off in a better direction instead. We should never let pridefulness, a fear of embarrassment, or inertia keep us on a course that we begin to discern is wrong for us. Life often presents us with new twists and turns, unexpected developments, and even occasional reversals of direction. The most successful people are led by instinct, intuition, and inspiration, that little voice that warns, and a sense of calling that guides them to choose proper goals most of the time, and then to make any corrections that are needed along the way.

We should never allow ourselves to wallow in regret about any inappropriate goals we have pursued. We need to learn and move on. As preferable as it is to avoid a false path in the first place, a few missteps can often show us where the right road lies. Sometimes the problems, difficulties, and even disasters that result from seeking the wrong things can wake us up to what we need.

Adversity is the midwife of genius.

Napoleon (1769–1821)

It's not just setting goals that is so important. It's setting the right goals. Learn from your mistakes. This is part of the inner art of goal conception. Then do what you can to go and sin no more.

CHAPTER

A Vivid Vision

3

Every art depends on imagination. The art of goal setting—our inner conception of what to pursue—is no exception. Our goals should be firmly rooted in the fertile soil of the imagination to be connected with the deepest sources of motivation we have. Too many people set goals intellectually but omit doing so with the power of their innermost vision.

FANTASY AND DESIRE

Why do so many New Year's resolutions and other self-improvement programs so quickly fade and end in defeat? For a very simple reason. To explain, let me make some crucial philosophical distinctions, beginning with the notions of fantasy and desire.

Fantasy

This is the realm in which most of our New Year's resolutions and "new me" programs actually dwell.

I have a fantasy of spending all the rest of my days lying on a beach in the Bahamas, doing nothing morning, afternoon, and night. But to my surprise, I have to admit that if I were suddenly offered the opportunity tomorrow, I'd turn it down. There are too many things I want to do that are incompatible with the implications of my fantasy. Its reality would preclude other things I truly want.

How many of our daydreams
would darken into nightmares
if there seemed any danger of their coming true!
Logan Pearsall Smith (1865–1946)

In realizing that I wouldn't accept the substance of a particular daydream if it were actually offered to me, I become aware that this fantasy is nothing more than a mere passive figment of my imagination. It is not a real desire.

Desire

A simple fantasy is one thing, a desire is something stronger.

A fantasy is a shimmering fiction, a typically pleasant image lying inert in the imagination. A desire is a matter of the appetites, broadly construed. It is an inclination of the will.

A desire is connected to volition, our capacity for choice, as an influence, a tendency, or a leading force, however weak or strong. It goes beyond the range of mere imagination. It is possible to fantasize something you don't really desire, like my Bahamian life of leisure. And that's possible only because the fantasy is built on component desires, yet goes beyond them. I do desire time for relaxation, sunshine, proximity to the ocean, and an occasional tropical drink. What I don't desire is the whole package as an exclusive, uninterrupted lifelong deal.

You can indeed fantasize about something you don't really desire. It's also possible to desire something you have never fantasized. I desire a cup of coffee right now, and I have often had the desire for one, but I have never fantasized it. Some of you coffee fiends may have, but I'm sure you can find your own examples of the distinction. Fantasy and desire are just different.

His own desire leads every man.

Virgil (70–19 B.C.)

The important point is that a fantasy doesn't necessarily translate into a desire. It's possible to have a dream that never gets ahold of the will at all, and so never becomes a desire. Some announcements of New Year's resolutions and new-me programs are just revelations of fantasy. They never get off the ground because they never get any grip on the will.

But even when the will is involved, as in the case of a desire, something more is needed than mere influence or inclination if there is to be a significant chance of real change. A further distinction must be made. It's possible to have a desire, even a strong one, that never reaches the status of a goal.

Goal

A fantasy is a dream, a desire is an inclination, a goal is a commitment of the will.

This point is so important and so overlooked that I want to say it again, with feeling: A goal is a commitment of the will. You never have a goal without a real commitment.

Desires often just come upon us. If we acted to satisfy all of them, our lives would be a mess. Some of our desires are fleeting, but pursuing them would do permanent damage. Some would lead to situations that would not be good for us. Many would have consequences that would not be good for people we care about. We have to learn which of our desires to pursue and which to resist. This is part of the often difficult task of acquiring wisdom in life.

A desire is an influence on choice, but a goal is the result of a choice. What you have chosen to pursue is your goal. It's not just a fantasy. It's not just a desire. It's a selected target, the determinant of a chosen direction, which gives guidance and direction to your subsequent choices.

A goal is never inert. If you are not moving in the direction of losing weight, you haven't really taken weight loss as a goal. Not yet. If you're not moving in the direction of financial independence, then that's not really one of your present goals. It may be a fantasy. It may be a desire. But it's not yet a goal.

Too many New Year's resolutions and other "decisions" to make changes for the better fail to make any real difference in our lives because they never get out of the realms of fantasy or desire and achieve the true status of a goal, a genuine commitment of the will.

Will is the measure of power.
Proclus (ca. 410–485)

GOALS AND THE IMAGINATION

Goal setting must be an act of the will that engages the whole person. It can never be just an intellectual exercise. Powerful goal setting needs to involve intellect, will, desire, emotion, and imagination.

Once you take something as a goal, once you make that commitment of the will, you should then work backward through the progression we have just been discussing. Make sure to cultivate supporting desires that will facilitate reaching that goal. Resist and uproot desires that will make it more difficult to hit your target.

But how can you do that? By moving all the way back to the realm of the imagination and making your goals imaginatively vivid. Put your imagination to work. Linked to goals, it can be a great source of power. The imagination can be used to get our emotions going, to make us truly care, to motivate us to draw on the deepest and most enduring resources we have. Without its help, we'll not likely have the power to overcome any difficulties we may encounter along the way. But with its support, it's amazing what we can accomplish.

Here is an interesting and welcome correlation: The bigger and more exalted our goals are, the more difficulties we are likely to face in pursuing them. But the bolder our goals are, the easier it is to engage the support of the imagination. So where we most need the imagination's help, we are most likely to get it. The bolder our vision is, the more imaginative our grasp of it in vivid detail, the easier it will be to marshal the power to deal with any obstacles to its realization that we may face along the way.

Make no little plans;
they have no magic to stir men's blood,
and probably themselves will not be realized.
Daniel Hudson Burnham (1846–1912)

The most powerful example I've ever seen of this was in the life of one of my students during my years of teaching at Notre Dame. On Monday, January 27, 1992, I walked into the Hesburgh Library Auditorium for the second full week of a freshman class, Philosophy 101, and in that three-hundred-seat room, two chairs were empty. One of my students was dead and the other, we were told, was paralyzed for life. On the previous Thursday evening, coming back in a snow storm from a swim meet, the bus carrying the women's swim team had crashed on the Indiana Toll Road three miles from the Notre Dame exit. Two of the young swimmers died, and one was informed she would probably never walk again. Haley Scott was paralyzed from the waist down. There was no movement in her lower body at all. The attending physician said there wasn't a chance in a million she would regain movement and have anything resembling a normal life. With a broken back, she was lucky to be alive at all.

But Haley wouldn't believe it. The doctors finally stopped telling her what she could never do again because they realized that she refused to listen. She said, "I always knew I would swim again." Every day after the negative diagnosis, she used her imagination vividly, envisioning what her first returning race would be like. She would picture the start, her stroke, the turn, the last effort to the finish, and touching the wall. Fantasy, desire, and will came together. Operation after operation, metal rods in her back, terrible pain—nothing could stop her inner quest for the goal of returning to competitive swimming.

Twenty one months later, as the Fighting Irish hosted a Midwestern Collegiate Conference swim meet, she found herself back in the Rolf's Aquatic Center pool at Notre Dame, swimming with all her might in the second heat of the fifty-yard freestyle event. She touched the wall, just as she had imagined again and again, ahead of the seven other swimmers, and won her first competitive heat since that horrible accident. It was a day of triumph and joyous tears that was never supposed to be.

This young woman marshaled everything within her to pursue her goal. The imagination in service to the will, buttressed by all her desires, brought her through horrendous pain. With an almost unimaginable effort, against enormous odds, she performed a feat that her emergency-room physicians would later call "truly miraculous."

Imagination is more important than knowledge.

Albert Einstein

I later saw Haley stand straight and tall and walk gracefully to a podium in the middle of the basketball arena at a huge Notre Dame football pep rally as thousands of people rose to their feet, applauding with all their might, and shouting out her name. She had proved to the Notre Dame family—and, through the national media, to the world—how the indomitable spirit of a human being with dreams and will can overcome and conquer the worst of adversities, with the greatest of results. Even for those of us who will never be challenged by anything like Haley's struggle, this is an extraordinarily important lesson to learn.

SPREADING YOUR VISION

In business contexts, executives and team leaders often make a serious mistake. When bold, demanding new goals are being set, they too often appeal just to the intellects of their associates with numbers, statistics, graphs, and charts of all kinds. They preach, exhort, cheerlead, and try to motivate. But they fail to draw sufficiently on the deepest source of motivation which alone has the power they need to harness: the imaginations of the people who are to do the job.

Only when we engage the imagination do we touch people's deepest hopes and fears, their highest aspirations, and their most fundamental determination. We can do this in a variety of ways, but one of the most powerful involves the basic and ancient art of storytelling.

If you are in a leadership or management position and need to set for others some tough new goals, you must first ask yourself: Have I imagined vividly enough the pursuit of these new goals, and the positive results of attaining them? Have I also imagined by contrast where we'll end up if we don't move in this direction and settle for less instead? Fire sparks fire. Only a lively, vivid imagination working within you can prepare you to evoke the same in others.

For it is feeling and force of imagination that makes us eloquent.

Quintillian (ca. 35–ca. 100)

Once you are worked up imaginatively and emotionally, then tell the story to your coworkers. Help your associates catch the vision. Don't be afraid to show your emotion. Business is not a cool function of the detached intellect trying to make antiseptic contact with the unmoved will. Business is passion pursuing excellence. It is energy and emotion put into the service of intelligent, heartfelt planning. Business is people together testing their skills, their strength, and their will to succeed for the good of all involved. And this can be brought to the most meaningful, satisfying level of excellence only if everyone's imagination is fully engaged.

Men, as well as women, are much oftener led by their hearts than by their understandings.

Philip Stanhope, earl of Chesterfield (1694–1773)

Lead by your heart and by your head. Lead your own life down the paths you choose with the lure of imaginative vision, and you can lead others the very same way.

I hope you never face the magnitude of challenge that Haley Scott confronted. But I hope that, whatever you do encounter in your life and work, you are able to bring together imagination, desire, and will in pursuit of your highest goals. Positive imagination, supporting desire, and the power of a committed will give us the greatest foundation for achievement in all areas of our lives.

CHAPTER

4 Purpose and Growth

The first of the seven universal conditions of success tells us that in every new challenge and in every enterprise we need a clear *conception* of what we want, a vivid vision, a goal clearly imagined. Thus, the first of the seven arts of success is the art of conceiving proper goals. To make sure our goals are right for us, we need an overall sense of mission and purpose in our lives.

THE BIG PICTURE

A conviction of mission or purpose directing our lives in the broadest possible way gives us a sense of meaning in our activities and relationships. This is one of the deepest, most important, and most underrated goods that can enter a life. We all want to be well paid for our work. We want to be liked and appreciated for what we do. But perhaps the deepest human need is to have a sense of meaning in our endeavors, and in our lives. Meaningful work will more likely be done well. A meaningful life is one that makes sense, in its goals, plans, and actions, because of a big picture that brings with it purpose and direction. We all need a big picture for our lives and work, a framework for properly directed goal setting.

For whatever we do ought to be in harmony with this:
No man can set in order the details unless he has already
set before himself the chief purpose of his life. . . .
The reason we make mistakes is because we all
consider the parts of life, but never life as a whole.
Seneca

All specific goals should be motivated by an overall sense of meaning and purpose. "Why am I doing this?" "Why does this matter?" If we can't answer the why question in a way that ultimately connects with our deepest sense of meaning or purpose, a particular goal may not be right for us to pursue. My own sense of purpose has come to be centered on family and philosophy: I want to nurture a strong family life and, with that base, bring practical wisdom into as many other people's lives as I can. Any goal I consider setting has to be tested by that twofold purpose of family and philosophy. If it's not consistent with my sense of purpose, I shouldn't pursue it. Without a touchstone like this, any of us can end up going in directions we later regret.

Specific goals should also ideally be associated with a standard for measuring progress and success. Some people go too far and seem to believe, "If you can't measure it, it isn't important." That's certainly an unhealthy extreme, because many human values don't allow easily for any sort of straightforward quantification and measurement. But for the most part, while acknowledging the reality and importance of the unmeasurable aspects of life, we still should do whatever we can to link as many of our particular goals as possible to some yardstick for measuring the results of our efforts. Otherwise, we'll never be sure when we need to change our methods, speed up, slow down, or adopt alternative goals instead. In addition, being able to see measurable progress while we are still far short of a target provides continued motivation. When a difficult goal is right for us to have, seeing real progress along the way provides ongoing confirmation that we're using our energies productively.

A big picture gives purpose and direction to our goal setting, and then our goals themselves give purpose and direction to all our actions relevant to them. Our sense of direction in life, in a relationship, or at work will guide our imaginations and give rise to a particular vision for our days. It's certainly possible to change direction in life, but we change direction, and change our overall purposes, much less often than we alter our goals within those purposes that we embrace. This is a fundamental aspect of the art of inner goal conception.

GROWING A LIFE

All that is human must retrograde if it does not advance.
Edward Gibbon (1737–1794)

In this life, we're either getting better or we're getting worse. If we're not growing, we're diminishing. When we're not heading forward, we're slipping back. This is true physically, intellectually, spiritually, and in all our relationships. Wherever we are in our lives, or in our work, improvement is needed. Not just when things are unacceptable, but also when things are good. The good should always give way to the better. Otherwise, it will at some point inevitably dissipate into the worse.

When we've been successful, when we've set goals and met them, when we feel that we've attained an admirable level of accomplishment, we must beware of a danger we always face: the lure of self-satisfied complacency. The danger of failing amid success to see that we need to set new goals to pursue, perhaps even very new goals. When one pursuit has come to a successful conclusion, another new one should begin. Life is supposed to be a series of adventures. One always should lead to the next.

We must always change, renew, rejuvenate ourselves;
otherwise we harden.
Goethe (1749–1832)

Let me quote the business writer Tom Peters on this. In a lively conversation he once remarked, "The one thing I believe for sure is that success kills. It leads to conservatism and arrogance. You don't even have to get arrogant. Conservative is enough."

When things are good, we become set in our ways. We easily take too high a view of ourselves for our past accomplishments and become less able to see changes we still need to make for the future. As the ancient philosopher Heraclitus (ca. 540–480 B.C.) famously proclaimed, things are always changing. What worked brilliantly last year may fall flat today. What succeeds today may fail next month. If we become too self-assured, we lose the humility that facilitates openness to learning what's needed now. If we become too conservative, we hesitate to adopt new goals or new procedures for achieving them.

A good thing which prevents us from enjoying
a greater good is in truth an evil.
Spinoza (1632–1677)

One of the greatest companies I have served as a philosopher once experienced this phenomenon in a very public way. They had long been the giant in their industry, the paradigm, the standard of excellence against whom all competitors were measured. They were so good at what they did that they didn't pay sufficient attention to new ways of doing business that were being created by rapidly advancing technologies. They weren't geared to fast adaptation and change on a big scale, but this had never seemed to matter precisely because they were so successful. When the pace of technological change and opportunity increased to such an extent that they came to be perceived as measurably behind the pack, they started to lose some very good people to competitors who already had been adopting the new technologies and creating innovative ways of doing business.

Fortunately, this great company has come to see the cost of complacency and has made heroic efforts to catch up, but the lag time did have an impact on their reputation and their ability, over the short run, to recruit and retain the best people. It needn't be arrogance or smugness that has this effect. It can be just the natural mind-set of successful people confident in the continued efficacy of what's worked in the past. But it's the opposite of the attitude we need for proper growth.

THE ENEMY OF THE BEST

We've long known that the good is often the enemy of the best. When things are awful, we're goaded into change. When our situation is intolerable, we have little trouble taking action. We seek improvement and are willing to work hard at it. But when things are good—well, hey, everything's fine.

In human affairs, the best stimulus for running ahead
is to have something we must run from.
Eric Hoffer (1902–1983)

If there's nothing bad to run from, what's going to get us off our duffs and goad us into moving ahead with new goals and a new sense of purpose? Well, guess what? There's always something to run from. The Decline. The Diminution. The Stagnation. The Big Backward Slide. The good that's the enemy of the best.

Here's an important lesson. Suppose you're out in the woods for a hike. You're surrounded by hilly terrain. Imagine that you're leading a group of people. Together, you set it as your goal to get to the top of the highest hill around where you'll have the best view possible of all that's in the area. Spotting a hill that seems to tower above the rest, you begin your climb. After a long ascent, you finally make it to the top. You feel a natural sense of accomplishment. But then suddenly you realize that, from where you stand, you're now able to see a significantly higher nearby peak previously blocked from view by the hill you've just climbed.

If your goal is to get to the highest point in the area, and you now realize you're on the second-highest peak, what's the first thing you'll have to do in order to achieve your goal? The answer is simple. You'll have to go downhill. You'll have to descend from the hill you're on in order to climb the higher one.

As the leader, it's your job to inform everyone else that you need to go back downhill. They followed your leadership up this first hill. They worked and struggled and finally arrived at the top. They've celebrated and relaxed, and are now enjoying the view. Can you imagine the reaction? "Hey! What do you mean? You're taking us downhill? Why? We're fine! We're up really high. We can see all we need to see from right here. It took a lot of work to get here. Where we are already is good. Let's just stay."

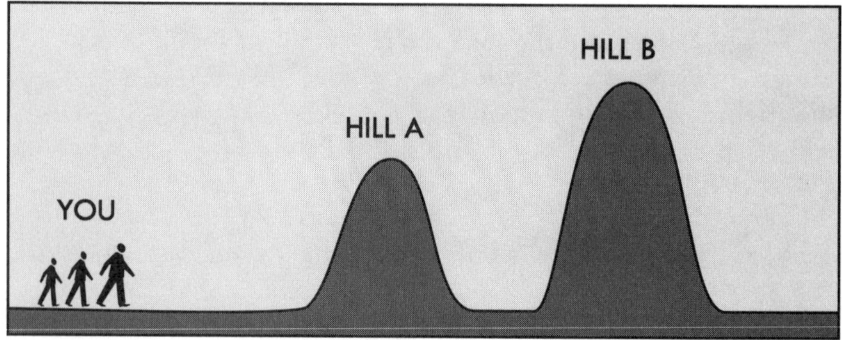

We have here the difference between a local maximum and a global maximum. On the peak you've first surmounted, you're at a local maximum. But you're not at a global maximum. From where you now stand, you can see that. You also can see that the initial stage of any effort at improvement will make your situation temporarily look worse compared to your ultimate goal. The fact is that you have to go downhill first in order to get to the higher mountain.

I walk firmer and more secure uphill than down.
Montaigne (1533–1592)

Going downhill metaphorically represents changing what you have been doing. It means doing something new and different. And for many people, making any major change at all is a bitter pill. Too many businesses, families, and individuals are stuck on the first good hill they climb. They've always done things one way. They're comfortable with where they are. Things seem fine. They don't want to go downhill. But in this life, there is always a higher hill to climb, one that will give us a greater vantage point, and a greater sense of accomplishment than anything we've yet felt. We can't experience that unless we are prepared first to go downhill.

Throughout the centuries, wise people have urged us not to let what is very good keep us from what is best. We can learn to enjoy each of our accomplishments, and savor every step of the journey we have taken so far, while still preparing for the next adventure we need to take. We can't let inertia hold us back. Progressing to greater heights sometimes means being prepared to go downhill temporarily.

One executive recently told me about changing over computer systems in his business. He said he had never heard people complain so much about anything. They were saying the old system worked fine. They knew how to use it. Now they were spending enormous amounts of time just trying to master the basics of the new system. He kept hearing "Things were fine! Why are we doing this?"

The office had been at a local maximum. And the employees felt like everything was okay there. They were comfortable. They saw no need for change. Nothing was bad. Everything was good. They were almost defeated by the enemy of the best.

The management team had to work hard to persuade everyone that after an initial "period of adjustment" (translation: royal pain), things would end up going much better than ever. The new system would simplify a number of procedures and allow them all to do new important things, if they would just make the change and hang in there during the brief initial downhill phase. This is often what's required for positive growth. Beware of the Downhill Blues.

There is no fruit that is not bitter before it is ripe.
Publilius Syrus (ca. 85–43 B.C.)

Sometimes we ourselves have an inner sense that it's time for a change. At other times, the world points it out to us. What has been very successful in the past may start to become less so. We may face hurdles or run into dead ends we haven't experienced before. At the same time, a new opportunity may begin to present itself. This is often the way life guides us into new opportunities. We need the flexibility of mind not to assume that tomorrow's success must have the same form as yesterday's, any more than we think your success should have the same form as mine.

A physician friend decided he wanted to quit his nephrology practice to go and study ethics and philosophy. He informed his partners he would be leaving, and continued to work while his patients were being transferred to other specialists. He told me he had been approached several times in the hospital parking lot by other doctors who came up and greeted him with a smile and the words "I hate you." When he asked why, they inevitably said, "You're doing what I want to do and can't do." Again, he asked why. The response was always that other people's expectations, their own sense of comfort, or a lifestyle that pushed to the edge of their incomes dictated that they stay right where they were. They had become enslaved to habits of consumption, habits of thought, and assumptions about what counts as success in life. Nobody wanted to be labeled a "quitter." No one could walk away and face the possible difficulties of starting something new.

CHOOSING A PATH

When you're feeling healthy, it's hard to launch into a physical improvement program. Whenever I've begun a new exercise routine of weight training, or sit-ups, or running, I soon feel much worse. I'm sore, achy, and I'm even feeling weaker than before I started. This is the short downhill phase, during which I'm hardly a specimen of fitness. It's difficult to keep it up. It's tough to make any change that involves initial difficulty when things were appearing just fine as they were. But, as Plato taught us, appearances and realities are often quite different things.

I'm speaking from personal experience in many ways here. I spent fifteen wonderful years at the University of Notre Dame, where I had great students, met fascinating people, learned like crazy, won unexpected teaching awards, and was able to be part of one of the most extraordinary educational enterprises in America. It was very good for me and my family. Yet, gradually, I began hearing a call to move on, to teach and learn in a different context, to go and pioneer new ways of being a philosopher in the modern world.

Why should I even have thought about a change? What could there possibly have been to run from, or leave behind, in a situation like that? Maybe stagnation. Possibly a diminution of growth. Perhaps the trap of becoming so comfortable amid success that my ability to hear any call to move on to a new goal and new opportunity may have begun to atrophy.

Growth is the only evidence of life.
John Henry Newman (1801–1890)

Some of us quite properly stay with the same organization or do the same job for our entire working careers. Our personal growth will occur within those parameters. We all have limits within which we develop and contribute to our world. But in another sense, our growth in principle can be endless within those structures of talent and calling that are distinctively ours.

Should a good job be left behind because, maybe, it's the enemy of the best? Should a good marriage be abandoned because, who knows, there could possibly be a better match out there? Not at all. I'm not suggesting this for a minute. Something's being good is not a sign that it should be temporary. That would be a perverse point of view. It's just that we always need to be careful that we not react to goodness with the response of inertia and prematurely stop our growth in any area of life. Even though I always need to be growing as a person, I didn't always need to be growing as a university professor. My growth in that capacity was to continue only as long as continuing in that capacity was best for my overall growth. In fact, I believe that we have discovered here a somewhat convoluted but extremely important eternal truth: Our growth in any capacity is to continue only as long as continuing in that capacity is best for our overall growth. Ponder that one.

LIMITED-OPTION THINKING

Too many people are held back from the adventures they should be living by limited-option thinking. One version of this form of thinking is the common conception of success as a straight-line phenomenon. The successful newspaper columnist is expected to achieve syndication, and then eventually to write a book. If that book is successful, the next step in accomplishment is naturally to write another book, preferably better than the first, and with even bigger sales. And so on and on. Success breeds straight-line expectations, and this can limit the challenges we seek. We see the same thing in every domain of life.

Think of the young TV personality who doesn't grow up to be a mature star of stage or screen. Is he a failure? We should never assume so. Life just may have had a different adventure for him. The person with two hit movies need not ever make a third or fourth. A rock guitarist may decide to sell real estate. Or open a bookstore. Or go to medical school. Or teach. The syndicated columnist may write just one book and then start raising chickens. Straight-line success can be wonderful, and it can be fulfilling, but we have to realize that it's not the only game in town.

The absurd man is he who never changes.
Auguste Barthélémy (1809–1876)

In many ways we have far too simplistic a view of success in our culture. You may have been successful at some particular activity for the past five years, but that need not imply that if you don't do the very same thing, or some standard natural derivative of it, successfully this year or next year, you have suddenly become a failure or a has-been. Instead, you may just now be launching out into a new adventure and moving toward some new form of success.

Is this a universal cop-out? Are we just redefining success and failure so that, under the banners of personal growth or adventure, any abandoning of an activity is just potential success in a new one? No, not at all. Not every new opportunity is a good one. Not everyone who changes direction does so well. Not every switch of course is a contribution to personal growth. But some are. Success in one thing, at one stage of life, should never be unduly confining. The truth is that your personal growth may require liberation from one successful enterprise in order to allow the beginning of a very new kind of quest and, potentially, an even greater success.

The high strength of men knows no content with limitation.
Aeschylus

A graduate student contemplating a very difficult upcoming exam was worrying aloud in my presence. He said, "I have to pass this exam. I can be only a philosophy professor or a house painter—and I really hate painting houses." I'm happy to report that he did pass the exam, receive his Ph.D., and become a professor. The world didn't need a new house painter who hated his job.

This student's comment about the upcoming exam was a classic example of limited-option thinking. Where in the world did a highly intelligent individual come up with such a view—that there were only two possible life scenarios for him? He was letting past experience dictate the future. He had been paid in the past only for teaching and painting. So an inertial thought process unconsciously convinced him that those were his only two options.

Why is it that we seem to define ourselves and what we can do with our lives only by what we are currently doing, or by what we've done in the past?
Joan Lunden (b. 1950)

Limited-option thinking is one of the main enemies of personal growth and true success in the world today. Our choices are always broader than our past. The best adventures in life need to be chosen, not from a predetermined menu based on what we've done already, but rather out of our own deepest sense of who we are and how we can contribute to the world. Again, a sense of mission and purpose should lead the way. We sometimes have to leave the comfort of what we know for opportunities that lie partially in the domain of the unknown.

An important related point needs to be made. Choosing a path of personal growth should not be thought of as necessarily the same thing as choosing whether to continue in or leave a particular job. Professional growth is just a part of personal growth. And what's best for a person's overall growth is not always the same thing as what's best for his or her professional development. Career development, or job-related growth, is just one dimension of personal growth, and should never eclipse all else. This is a great danger at our period of social and economic history.

Another point is just as important. Personal growth should never be understood as being opposed to the growing and deepening of our relationships. An important part of personal growth consists in what we learn and what we become as we interact in positive ways with a spouse, our children, or other relatives and friends. Part of it can happen through our struggle to understand and deal with difficult people at work. The person who quits jobs and abandons people just to chase "growth" is not a paradigm of positive human development. Nor, however, is a person who allows himself to continue on in patterns of work and life that are diminishing, or increasingly detrimental, in their overall impact. We are constantly called upon to choose what to preserve and what to change in our lives. Choice often isn't easy. But it is necessary.

The strongest principle of growth lies in human choice.
George Eliot (1819–1880)

With a strong sense of purpose, a big picture for our lives, and a conviction that what is very good should not keep us from seeking what is best, we put ourselves in a position to envision and choose new paths of rewarding adventure, new journeys of the heart and mind that can enrich who we are and increase our contribution to the world. This is the path of true success.

PART 2

THE ART OF CONFIDENCE

The great end of art is to strike the imagination with the power of a soul that refuses to admit defeat even in the midst of a collapsing world.

Friedrich Nietzsche (1844–1900)

CHAPTER

The Power of Belief

5

CONDITION 2 OF THE 7 CS:

*We need a strong **Confidence** that we can attain our goal.*

There's one blessing only,
the source and cornerstone of beatitude—
confidence in self.
Seneca

It's hard to believe in yourself when you're not sure you know what you're doing. And in times of tremendous change, how often do any of us feel really confident that we know exactly what we're doing? Sometimes it can seem as though we're skating on the thinnest possible ice, or groping through the dark, blindfolded. Just when we begin to feel the first glimmerings of confidence, when we become a little comfortable with how things are going, *boom!* Change grabs us by the collar once again and spins us around. We're reeling. "What's this?" New territory all over again. And the new enterprise jitters.

The greatest philosophers have thought that we should expect the world to pose us a series of challenges. They have known that challenges can be unnerving. So they've reminded us of the vital importance of working on self-confidence in everything we do. They also have left us a great deal of wisdom to draw on concerning the second ancient art of success, the art of confidence building.

CONFIDENCE AND COURAGE

Whenever we launch out into a new endeavor, it's natural to be a bit nervous, somewhat worried, a little unsure. It's a mark of intelligence. I once had two dogs—Bucky, a shepherd-collie mix, and Roo, a German short-hair–Pointer–blue tick hound–heinz 57 combo. Every time we took them to the vet, Bucky got nervous. Roo wagged his tail. Bucky was highly intelligent. Roo was sweet, but dumb as a stick. The vet pointed out to us that this is usually how it goes: Smart dogs worry about the experience. The intellectually challenged just wag right into it.

Stupidity is without anxiety.
Goethe

The same thing seems to be true of human beings. The more intelligent you are, the more you may tend to worry. You anticipate all the possibilities of trouble. As Aristotle, no wagger himself, put it, there are a great many ways to go wrong, and just one way to get anything exactly right. There are lots of ways to miss a bull's-eye, and just one spot where you hit it dead center. Many falsehoods can vie to substitute for any truth.

It takes a smart person to understand fully the risk involved in any new endeavor and to master the fine art of worry. It often takes a supreme exercise of intellect to see when and how that worry should be overcome. Anxiety shouldn't block our path to success. But it should make us more observant as we move forward.

Always it comes about that the beginning of wisdom is a fear.
Miguel de Unamuno y Jugo (1864–1936)

Anxiety, and even fear, can play a strong positive role in human life. Anxiety is often what makes us slow down and take care in what we're doing. It can be our guide to minimizing unnecessary risk and maximizing the long-term sustainable use of our resources. And fear, which we usually think of as a bad thing, can give rise to caution, which we normally think of as a good thing. Fear can even give rise to wisdom. But wisdom can arise out of fear only if we properly respond to it. We must not allow such negative emotions to control us and prevent our proper success.

Handling matters of fear and confidence is, like almost anything else, an issue of balance. The human being who rarely feels fear, anxiety, or worry may be insensible to risk, and because of that can be in danger of acting in a foolhardy or imprudent manner. On the other end of the spectrum, people who can't ever set aside their worries and muster confidence for worthwhile ventures never experience the success they deserve in life.

Our friend Aristotle has given us a general formula for all virtues, or character strengths, in human beings: A virtue is the midpoint between two vices, and these vices are opposite extremes on a spectrum. For example, the virtue of courage is the midpoint on a spectrum of ways to respond to danger:

The rash person is in some way blind to danger. The coward is blinded by it. The courageous person is intelligent enough to recognize risk, but committed enough to act despite it, when action is appropriate.

The mind which knows how to fear, knows how to go safely.
Publilius Syrus

There is nothing to be ashamed of in feeling fear or worry when launching into a very new enterprise. Any properly cognizant and sensitive person will feel a twinge of trepidation. This doesn't detract from an individual's courage in the least. A courageous person is not one who is unaware of danger or unmoved by it; a person of courage is one who, despite the downward pull of uncertainty, is able to reach upward and march forward toward a worthwhile goal.

Fortune favors the brave.
Terence (ca. 190–160 B.C.)

The individual brave enough to launch out in action despite the possibility of failure is the type of person most likely to succeed in our world. Inaction rarely accomplishes much except when it's a temporary stage of patient waiting in an overall plan of action. And even patience often requires courage and confidence. Patience isn't always for the timid.

I should clarify the relationship between confidence, the focus of our second condition of success, and courage, which we've just been discussing. Courage is the ability and willingness to act despite danger. Confidence is an attitude of trust undergirding a belief in success. It might look at first as if courage and confidence are alternatives to each other as well as to fearful inaction: If you're very confident of success, you may not have to be very courageous; likewise, if you're very courageous you may not need to be very confident before taking action.

It's certainly possible to be courageous without being confident, when you bravely do what you think is right despite a perceived likelihood that you'll fail to secure your intended goal, or even your own safety in the process. It's also possible to be confident without having to be courageous, when you simply believe that you will succeed at something involving very little risk. But where success depends on a faith in yourself and is undertaken against a background of significant perceived risk, confidence and courage both can and must go hand in hand. In many situations, an attitude of confidence is the result of some degree of personal courage.

Confidence is that feeling by which
the mind embarks in great and honorable courses
with a sure hope and trust in itself.
Cicero

You may need some courage to undertake the actions necessary for generating the confidence you need. And you may need at least an initial confidence that courage is the right response to the situation in which you find yourself. As often as courage leads to confidence, a little act of confidence on your part, however manufactured, can be just what you need to strengthen the courage you're mustering to face a new challenge. A dose of confidence and a touch of courage often make for a powerful partnership.

Make no mistake about it. You can be both a courageous person and a cautious person, and it may be this very caution that in part undergirds the rationality of a courageous response to your situation. Caution can actually contribute to confidence. A careful approach to any challenging situation will help you avoid many of the potential obstacles that might otherwise thwart your progress. So in stressing the importance of confidence to success, I would never urge rashness or blindness to either danger or difficulty. We need to have our eyes wide open as we move forward in pursuit of our goals.

Confident because of our caution.
Epictetus (ca. 55–135)

THE IMPORTANCE OF CONFIDENCE

Why is confidence one of the universal conditions of success? Isn't it possible to succeed at something while having very little confidence along the way? Isn't it possible to be surprised by your success? A confident person believes that things will work out well. A genuinely surprised person cannot really have believed that at all.

Of course, there are degrees of confidence and surprise, and they are inversely related. The more confident you are that a particular event will happen, the less surprised you'll be when it does happen. Conversely, the greater your surprise is, the less your confidence was. The very fact that it is indeed possible to be surprised by your own success shows that achievement is at least sometimes possible without having been preceded by a perfect, supreme confidence. And that's a good thing. It's fairly simple to nurture some measure of confidence in your mind and in the hearts and minds of your coworkers. But it's very difficult and extremely rare to be able to instill within anyone a maximal degree of positive belief in future outcomes.

Perfect confidence is not necessary for success. An exceedingly high degree of confidence is not a strict requirement for many kinds of achievement. But the more difficult a task is, the better positioned we are to handle it if we have a significant measure of initial confidence, or what the philosopher William James called "pre-cursive faith," faith that literally "runs ahead of," or goes beyond, the available evidence that we will indeed prevail.

The easier a task is, the less matters of confidence need to enter the equation. And, of course, it is possible for the improbable to happen, regardless of whether you have any confidence in its happening or not. But it is indeed improbable.

I'm not suggesting for a minute that confidence is a logically necessary condition for success, that it's strictly impossible to achieve anything without believing in yourself and the likelihood of your attaining your goals. You may be able to succeed at all sorts of things without a lick of confidence in your abilities. You can win the lottery without believing for a second that you actually would. Confidence is neither a strictly necessary condition for success nor a guarantee of it.

It's just one of the most important facilitating conditions of success that are within our control whenever we face a challenge. And it's one we often can employ in such a way as to raise the objective probability of success for our efforts.

Self-trust is the first secret of success.
Ralph Waldo Emerson

The attitude of confidence is an important facilitator of success for a variety of reasons. First, confidence in our abilities will launch us into action much more boldly. As we saw earlier, there are things to be learned in any venture that are accessible only when we are moving out into the world making things happen. Confidence gets us moving, keeps us moving, and positions us to learn.

Second, confidence allows a freer flow of our deepest energies and efforts to overcome challenges along the way that might squelch the initiative of a less confident person. Let's face it, the nobler and more exalted a goal is, the more difficult it usually will be to attain. Without a fairly strong confidence in what we're doing, we'll be less likely to persist in the face of defeat, discouragement, apparent failure, and postponed results. The history of worthwhile discoveries, inventions, and creative efforts is a history of trouble, hardship, and stubborn persistence through it all.

I think and think for months and years.
Ninety-nine times, the conclusion is false.
The hundredth time I am right.
Albert Einstein

There is also a third reason for the importance of confidence. Hardly anything worth doing in this world can be done by one person completely alone. Our best efforts usually bear fruit as a result of the supporting efforts of other people. When you stop to think about it, the network of relationships underlying any significant success is most often nearly mind-boggling. Just think of your own teachers, mentors, associates, friends, and acquaintances, along with the often crucial role they have played in positive things you've experienced. A star athlete depends on coaches, trainers, and teammates.

An actor depends on writers, directors, and producers, as well as on fellow cast and crew members. An executive depends on employees, and any salesperson relies on contacts and references. A healthy self-confidence and a strong faith in the prospects of your work will inspire those around you to give of themselves more wholeheartedly in what you are doing together. It's something like a universal psychological law: Confidence unleashes potential both in an individual and in a team.

To establish oneself in the world,
one does all one can to seem established there already.
François, duc de La Rochefoucauld (1613–1680)

When you begin to work with someone who seems not only talented and likable but also confident, how does this affect your attitude toward her and the likely success of your joint project? You're probably much more inspired and more enthusiastic about the task. You likely move forward with greater assurance yourself. Another person's confidence, or lack of confidence, can affect any of us deeply. Your own confidence can affect others the same way.

We've probably all seen this in action. A network television show once did a segment on successfully flirting with strangers in public places. The main advice was to act confident and look confident. Confidence, it seems, produces all kinds of success.

Have you ever read about famous party crashers, people who can get into almost any restricted event or party, backstage at the Academy Awards, in the dressing rooms of the stars of a rock concert, or even at private homes? Some of the stories are truly amazing. The ultimate example is perhaps the young Steven Spielberg, who walked onto the lot at Universal, found an empty office, and acted like he belonged there. Soon enough, he did. One thing all these stories have in common is the air of self-confidence displayed on the part of the person acting as though he or she deserves both deference and admission.

If a person affecting confidence can get in where he doesn't belong, imagine what this quality can do for a person who does belong, who's working on a legitimate and proper project.

There is a form of eminence that does not depend on fate;
it is an air that sets us apart and seems to portend great things;
it is the value that we unconsciously attach to ourselves;
it is the quality that wins us the deference of others;
more than birth, position, or ability, it gives us ascendance.

La Rochefoucauld

Confidence is attractive and can be quite contagious. Few people relish worry—although, admittedly, there are some. Most people lacking confidence in a venture they'd like to see succeed are looking for a reason to feel better about their prospects. If we are properly confident in what we're doing, we inspire the people around us to share that confidence and work with us for the results we all desire.

In praising confidence and extolling its attractiveness, I have to make it completely clear that I am not for a minute praising anything like arrogance or presumptuousness. Here again, Aristotle's model may be helpful. We can think of the virtue of proper confidence as the midpoint between two extremes on a spectrum of responses to uncertainty.

To go beyond is as wrong as to fall short.

Confucius (ca. 551–479 B.C.)

A virtuous confidence, a balanced healthy attitude of positive belief, can unlock the energies of your coworkers, team members, and business clients, just as it can free up your own talents and energies. Is it, then, important to success? I'm very confident it is.

CHAPTER

The Logic of Confidence

In any struggle to succeed at a new and difficult task, there's probably no psychological problem more common than a lapse of confidence. In my experience of working with people in nearly every kind of business, it seems to be one of most difficult to attain of The 7 Cs of Success. As you look around your office, and even your family, I bet you'll find your own experience in agreement with mine here. Why do people have such an extraordinarily hard time with this particular inner attitude?

If I have lost confidence in myself,
I have the Universe against me.
Ralph Waldo Emerson

There is a logic to having or lacking confidence. Understanding this logic is essential to any masterful practice of the art of confidence building. Logic and art are not, after all, opposed. Any problem of confidence can be diagnosed by the use of a logical array of possibilities, and then addressed by both logic and art.

THE CONFIDENCE CHECKLIST

To get a better handle on the problem of low confidence, and to gain some perspective on how we can begin to practice the crucial art of confidence building in any situation, let's look first at some of the deep foundations of this important attitude in human life.

Whenever we have confidence in a person, we believe that he will get the job done, or that she will succeed. When we believe in ourselves, we believe that we have what it takes and that we will achieve the goal we have set. And whenever we have confidence in ourselves or another person, the endpoint belief that we maintain is always of the form:

S will do X.

This in turn is always rooted in a more fundamental belief:

S can do X.

This in turn is dependent on a further series of beliefs:

Ability—S is able to do X.	**Capability—S is capable of doing X.**
S has the power to do X.	S is morally open to X.
S has the skill to do X.	S has the heart for X.
S has the opportunity to do X.	
S has the practical knowledge for X.	

These statements come close to being a complete analysis of the background beliefs for any case of confidence. They constitute a checklist for assessing the likelihood of finding confidence in a person, and for diagnosing lack of confidence so that we can do something about it.

The Forms of Ability

Power. This is one of the most fundamental concepts in philosophy, and for understanding the world. Power operates on many levels in human life. There is personal physical strength, political power, organizational power deriving from institutional status, and less formally instituted forms of interpersonal power. Any one or more of these might be relevant to a particular task or goal.

The same man cannot be well skilled
in everything; each has his special excellence.
Euripides (ca. 480–406 B.C.)

Skill. Skill is something like a cultivated, habitual form of "know-how," an ability to use the power you have in an effective way. It is typically the result of relevant experience. It is possible to be powerful without being skillful—we see this far too frequently in organizational life. And, although skill requires some degree of personal power for its cultivation, it is possible to have a skill level far exceeding your organizational power to act. A colleague can have the power to negotiate, but that doesn't guarantee he's skillful at it. Another associate could have the skill to negotiate contracts well without having been granted the organizational power to do so. So power and skill are different things and don't necessarily occur together.

Skill to do comes of doing.
Ralph Waldo Emerson

Opportunity. Opportunity is of course a matter of access. Is a person in the right place at the right time, or at least can he be? Does an individual's schedule and other commitments allow for the task to be undertaken and accomplished? Can a person position herself in such a way as to plug into the assistance needed to complete a project? These are all questions of opportunity.

A man must make his opportunity as oft as find it.
Francis Bacon

Practical knowledge. Practical knowledge is a form of understanding. When we ask whether a person has the degree of practical knowledge necessary for undertaking a particular assignment, we want to know whether, in the context of the opportunities available, she knows how to use the power and skill she has, to accomplish the task at hand. Practical knowledge ties the ability cluster of attributes together and makes them all realistically available for effective action. Practical knowledge could even be said to be a form of wisdom.

The Forms of Capability

Capability depends on what might be called, broadly speaking, "moral attributes." Even if a person has the power, skill, opportunity, and practical knowledge required to perform an action, he may be incapable of it if such an action were strictly forbidden by his formed moral character. A serious intention to do the thing could not arise or at least could not be maintained among his habitual tendencies to act. Some plants can't grow in some soil. In the same way, some people just can't do certain things. And that's a very positive fact about the world.

Moral openness. When we say of an evil person, "He's capable of anything," we mean that he has no stable moral character that would be incompatible with any evil intent or action. When we are wondering whether an individual will do a particular deed, one relevant consideration is whether he is morally open to it. If he is not, we should expect that he will not do it.

Having the heart. Sometimes a person is morally open to a task, and even has every quality in the ability cluster needed to do it, but just doesn't have the heart for it. By this I mean that the individual just can't muster either the will to initiate the task or the determination needed to see it through to completion. This seems to be a separate consideration when we determine whether a person can and will do something.

We have more ability than willpower, and it is often an excuse to ourselves that we imagine that things are impossible.
La Rochefoucauld

The announcement "It can't be done" is frequently a mask for "I don't feel like doing it" or "I can't be bothered to help." Often, people who don't have the heart for a job and don't want to admit that fact, even to themselves, will resist a new idea with the claim "It's impossible" or "It just won't work." We always have to be on guard for this little bit of misdirection in our own minds, and in the minds of those around us.

This, then, is the confidence checklist: ability and capability; power, skill, opportunity, practical knowledge, moral openness, and heart. When we want to assess our confidence in ourselves or in another person or her own confidence in herself, these are the touchstones. Does the individual have the ability and capability, and does she believe she does? Do I have what it takes? Am I convinced that I do?

THE DIAGNOSTIC APPLICATION

What is more mortifying than to feel that you have missed the plum for want of courage to shake the tree?
Logan Pearsall Smith

One of the most important things about the confidence checklist is that we can use it to diagnose any problem of confidence. Is a person at work struggling with worry and self-doubt? Am I experiencing some strong hesitation about a new direction that I'm taking? We just need to go through the Confidence Checklist to see exactly where the trouble might be. Is it an issue of power, of skill, of opportunity, or of practical knowledge? Or is it a worry on the broadly moral side of the checklist? When we can identify where the uncertainty is coming from, we can figure out how to deal with it.

If you're facing any problem of confidence, you may just need to get out some paper or turn on the computer and prepare to ask yourself some questions—and answer them.

1. *"Do I have the power to get the job done?"*

   If the answer is yes, then there's no problem on this score. If no, then ask yourself, "Can I acquire the power to get this job done?" or "Can I put together a team of people with the power needed?" A yes answer will establish a beachhead for confidence.

Consciousness of our powers augments them.
Luc, marquis de Vauvenargues (1715–1747)

2. *"Do I have the skill necessary for the task?"*

   If the answer is yes, then, again, no problem here. If no, then ask yourself, "Can I acquire the skill, or partner up with someone who has the skill needed?"

3. *"Do I have the opportunity to make this happen?"*

   If yes, notch up your confidence accordingly. If no, then ask, "Can I make the opportunity for myself that I need to get this done?"

4. *"Do I have the practical knowledge to put this together?"*

   If yes, then get moving. If no, then ask, "What do I have to do to get the practical knowledge needed here?"

5. *"Do I feel morally and ethically right about this project?"*

   If yes, then you don't have to be concerned about this sort of drain on confidence. If the answer is no, you must then ask yourself, "What do I need to do in order to clear up the ethics of the project?" If no good answer seems forthcoming, then it's appropriate to have a confidence problem. This may keep you from acting in such a way as to end up leaving you with a much bigger problem. If there's no ethical issue, go on to the next question.

6. *"Do I have the heart for this project, the will and determination to get it done?"*

   If you feel the answer is yes, then you've cleared the whole checklist. If no, then you have to ask, "What can I do to give myself the willpower and determination necessary for this?" If that answer is not something within your ability to accomplish in a reasonable time frame, then maybe you do need to change course. An identification of some clear measures to take here may be all you need for a positive resolution of this question.

At each step on the checklist, you are asking whether there is something you need to do along a particular dimension to position yourself to achieve success at the task you have chosen. If you have a sensible answer here for checklist item 6, as well as a positive result on all the other questions, you have all the information you need either to be sure you already have what it takes to get the job done, or to complete your preparation to do it. Any negative answers will have given you a diagnosis of where work is needed.

They can because they think they can.

Virgil

Let me highlight something that is often overlooked in a business setting. Whenever we have a high level of confidence in our undertaking of a task, X, we believe firmly:

X will happen as a result (at least in part) of our efforts.

But we believe this with strong confidence only when we also believe:

X is possible. We can make it happen.
X is permissible. It's not wrong for us to do it.
X is preferable. It is in some sense the best alternative we have.

These beliefs are positive responses to the simple questions:

Can X happen?
Is it okay for X to happen?
Is it best for X to happen?

We don't work confidently toward what we believe is impossible. What is often forgotten is that we also don't act very confidently to bring about something that we worry could be wrong, or even less preferable than some alternative. A strong confidence in what we're doing requires a conviction that our goal is attainable, that it's permissible, and that it's a preferred direction, from a prudential or a moral point of view. These last two issues map out some important territory that is not well enough understood, or at least acted on, by many executives in the world of business.

If we give the people who work with us new goals and want them to work confidently toward their achievement, we need to engage in a multiple-level confidence-building exercise. We should help them see that they already have, or else can acquire, the power, skill, opportunity, and practical knowledge it will take to get the job done. We need to do everything we can to convince them that the new goals are possible to achieve. But we also have to show that these goals are right to pursue, and that they're better than other paths we might take instead. We need to explain the big picture behind the setting of the new targets. What are the values behind these goals? Why was this strategy chosen rather than some alternative? How does it connect up with our overall sense of mission?

Look twice before you leap.
Charlotte Brontë (1816–1855)

Even considering these questions and how to give other people good answers to them brings to mind something important. To the extent that we can involve coworkers or associates in the process of arriving at new goals and not just deliver every one of them ready made and unalterable, we make it easier for everyone to buy in to those goals. Their values have been consulted, along with their sense of what they can accomplish. Then we won't face such a hard sell.

Of course, we'll often need to act as cheerleaders and work to build self-confidence in our associates. People are creatures of habit. Any new challenge is a stretch. And any such stretch produces the conditions under which doubts can arise and grow. But if we can excite our colleagues' imaginations in the right way, stretch their conceptions of what they can do, and better practice the art of confidence building, we will raise the objective probability of success in the new venture we share.

The power of belief is great and needs to be tapped more deliberately, as well as more regularly, in our efforts with other people. But first, of course, the art of building others' confidence requires that we deal with our own problems with lack of confidence, which we look at next.

CHAPTER

7 Cultivating Confidence

Nothing in the affairs of men
is worthy of great anxiety.
Plato (ca. 427–347 B.C.)

As I was finishing my first draft of the last chapter I heard my wife call up from downstairs, "Tom, plane crash! Turn on the TV!"

Nearly every week I'm flying someplace. Last week, Pebble Beach. This week, Dallas and St. Louis. Next week, Florida. After that, New York City. And I'm a guy who for seven years refused to get on an airplane. I had read too many crash stories, and I had let my imagination get too worked up about them. I figured this was one stress I could live—much longer—without. So I decided I'd never fly again. And I didn't, during seven active years of car trips, train rides, and a lot of just staying home, writing books and articles and visiting with people on the phone. But there are some good and important things you can't do if you don't fly. So now I fly, after going through a process of confidence building detailed in my 1994 book, *True Success.* But I fly carefully; I avoid airlines in trouble, types of planes about which questions have been raised, and small commuter planes flying in bad weather at night. And I can still use a little boost in my confidence now and then. Especially when I hear, still too often, those words from my wife.

CONFIDENCE BUILDING

On one recent flight, I sat next to a man who had flown fighter planes in Vietnam, a U-2 spy plane at over seventy thousand feet for twelve-hour stretches, and passenger jets for a major airline. He still worked in the aerospace industry, and so I figured he'd be an ideal person to question about air safety, as part of my ongoing confidence-building enterprise. So I asked him about commercial flight safety, and he gave me some interesting answers, leading off with the memorable line "Well, look, everybody's gonna die."

As you might imagine, that didn't do much for my confidence building. At first. But by the time I had once again landed safely—astonished—and had gotten to my hotel, I began to experience an important realization. My new friend's lead-off line was neither trivial nor fatalistically pessimistic. It was a reminder that can act as the basis for any courage-building or confidence-building exercise.

When we enter any new situation, engaged in a process that we have decided is right for us, and we encounter unexpected belief turbulence, we do well to ask ourselves: "What's the worst that could happen here?" And the answer we arrive at will demonstrate one of two things. Either that the worst that can possibly happen in the situation is not so bad after all, and so we can stop worrying about it, or that however bad the worst possible outcome seems, we can always put it into perspective by reminding ourselves that "everybody's gonna die" anyway. So even when we engage in an enterprise that carries a genuine risk of death, even a slight risk, as we do on a plane, in a car, or walking down the street, the worst that can happen is something that's definitely going to happen to us sometime someplace anyway. It's not as though we're going to be able to prevent it.

And that's somehow comforting. Not very, I have to admit. Yet it's a place to start.

In the long run, we are all dead.

John Maynard Keynes (1883–1946, as predicted)

Modern life in an advanced democracy in times of relative peace can be so wonderful. It's possible to live in such a way that you feel basically safe most of the time, which is another way of saying that it's possible to live under a deep illusion. We naturally crave safety. We need to feel some sense of stability and predictability about our lives. Yet comfort, stability, and predictability are sometimes just a smiley face plastered over stagnation. And stagnation is one of the worst plights for a human being. Playing it safe is often the riskiest thing we can do.

Only in growth, reform, and change,
paradoxically enough, is true security to be found.
Anne Morrow Lindbergh (1906–2001)

Change is the precondition for growth. It's also the precondition for a deep sense of fulfillment. Personally, I'm no fan of change for its own sake. I see no intrinsic good in going around always shaking things up and keeping people off guard. But I do understand that we are by nature dynamic creatures whose bodies and minds are undergoing changes all the time. We need a balance of stability and change in our lives to be happy. Too much change is not good. Too much stability is no better.

Some of the greatest rewards in this life tend to go to the people willing to make the newest plans, to those prepared to do something a little different and bold, to the originators of useful change. So the question we should ask is this: How can we build the confidence we need to make the kinds of changes in our lives and in our businesses that will yield the greatest rewards?

The most beaten paths are certainly the surest.
But do not hope to scare up much game on them.
André Gide (1869–1951)

There are really two different questions here. How can we become better at creating within ourselves goal-specific confidence? And how can we become generally more confident in all that we do?

INITIATING CHANGE

Let's look at the general issue first. It's hard for most of us to initiate change. And that's what launching out in the pursuit of any new goal is—initiating change. It's tough to do this because routine is one of the most durable security blankets in human life. We're all creatures of habit, and habit defines a comfort zone in our work as well as in our relationships. Yet change in our lives is both inevitable and ongoing.

Experiencing unwanted change is difficult. Typically, it's better to take some control of a situation and initiate your own change in a productive way when change is needed, or when it seems to be on the horizon. Some adventures in life will be thrust upon us. But we journey safest and with the most confidence when we take initiative and call as many of the shots as we can, planning the route we choose to travel into the territory ahead.

I believe that anyone can conquer fear
by doing the things he fears to do,
provided he keeps doing them until he gets
a record of successful experiences behind him.
Eleanor Roosevelt (1884–1962)

Most people don't seem to realize that change initiation is a skill just like tennis or golf. Nobody walks onto a tennis court or a golf course for the first time and plays like a champion. The relevant skills take time to develop. You probably won't even feel comfortable on the court or course at first. You have to log a lot of hours in front of the net or walking the links before it begins to feel like home.

It's the same with the skill of initiating change. We need to get used to it as a skill before we can overcome our fear of the new and feel comfortable with it. When people are promoted at work into decision-making positions that require a new level of initiative, I often advise them to do whatever they can, as soon as they can, to get their feet wet in making little decisions and setting small new goals for their department or office. Even some small changes at home or in their personal routines, of the most trivial sorts, can help loosen the perimeters of their individual comfort zones. They then can begin to develop a positive and necessary psychological adjustment to change. Gradually, this new openness becomes both a habit and a skill that paves the way toward a greater comfort level in dealing with bigger challenges. Your general confidence level always grows as you see yourself successfully initiating changes, however small, in any domain of your life.

Nothing so bolsters our self-confidence and reconciles us
with ourselves as the continuous ability to create;
to see things grow and develop under our hand, day in and day out.
Eric Hoffer

People who are accustomed to change in general tend to find themselves better able to cope with any particular change that comes their way. So if the people you work with avoid change because they dread disruption in their lives, it could be that they haven't initiated enough change successfully in the past, and they fear the unknown. You can help them recognize this as the way the human mind works, and ease them into a new dynamic attitude that's more comfortable with something new. Give them small changes and small victories to bolster their confidence. Then build to the bigger innovations you need to make.

Do not be too timid and squeamish about your actions.
All life is an experiment.
Ralph Waldo Emerson

On the general issue of confidence, this overall comfort with the initiation of change is the most important matter to be addressed. Remember too the philosophical insight that no one has been launched into this world for failure. We all need success, and we all have what it takes to attain our proper measure of it. Each of us has a special set of talents and experiences duplicated by no one else. As long as we're working with those talents and building on those experiences to do the kind of good we're in this world to do, we'll find ourselves operating with a higher confidence level than someone who has gotten off course, and properly doubts the appropriateness of their direction.

Skills vary with the man.
We must tread a straight path and
strive by that which is born in us.
Pindar (ca. 522–ca. 440 B.C.)

BUILDING CONFIDENCE FOR SPECIFIC GOALS

But now to the specifics. When we're working toward a particular goal, how can we increase our confidence level for that task? How can we help other people involved in the goal to do the same? There are several distinct methods for accomplishing this.

Inner Psyching

First is a set of techniques that we can use anywhere, anytime and that can have a strong positive effect on our level of confidence: *visualization, articulation,* and *positive self-talk.*

Visualization

Athletes are at the head of the class for using visualization techniques to build confidence and improve performance. A student who took two of my classes at Notre Dame became the number one college tennis player in the country by the time he graduated. He told me once that the practice of visualization had been the single most effective factor in getting his game to a higher level. He would vividly picture to himself in advance of a match exactly what he wanted to see happen in those games. And then he would go out and live the dream. This is an exercise of directed imagination, and it can have powerful results.

I've been told this more times than I can recall. The great Pittsburgh Pirates Hall of Famer Willie Stargell once recounted to me the many obstacles he had to overcome in his baseball career. People said he'd never make it to a major league team. He wasn't good enough. Then, when he proved them wrong, they said he surely wouldn't play much. He was up against too many great players. When he did get playing time, people told him to just do his job and forget dreams of home runs. Despite all the bad advice and gloomy prognostications of the naysayers, Willie maintained his focus and his belief in himself. One of his chief techniques for confidence building and implementation was to go into the locker room alone before a game, sit quietly, and visualize as vividly as he could the challenges and opportunities to come. He saw himself at bat and felt the powerful hit that sent the ball aloft. Then he'd go out and do it. By working on his inner confidence, along with his outer game, he ended up hitting 475 home runs while leading his team to two world championships as well as six National League Division titles.

Use your imagination not to scare yourself to death,
but to inspire yourself to life.
Adele Brookman

Visualization can be just as powerful in business and politics, medicine and law, working with children, solving crimes, performing music, and painting as it is in sports. It has great application potential in every department of life.

Articulation

Another former philosophy student of mine, Ricky Watters, a young and talented running back who made his name with the San Francisco

49ers, said that before Super Bowl XXIX, in 1995, he mentally saw himself making three touchdowns in the upcoming game. He then told other people about it. And in the game, he did exactly what he had seen and said.

Ricky was using not only the technique of visualization but also that of articulation. If we talk about or write about what we're planning to do, we use the power of language to accustom ourselves on a deep unconscious level to the results that we want. When we share our goals with others, we also tend to increase our level of commitment to make those goals actually happen. We've made it public. We've put it "out there" and now have something to live up to—in a sense, we've made a promise we need to keep.

We can talk ourselves into new levels of success, or into new forms of failure. It's up to us how we use this power of articulation. Great people use it to support their goals.

If you ask me what I came to do in this world,
I will answer you: "I am here to live out loud."
Emile Zola (1840–1902)

Talking or writing about what we're aiming at begins to move us and others into a new comfort level with what we're discussing. The power of articulation can be extraordinary in helping us to clarify our goals. It can also be unexpectedly powerful in creating within us the confidence we need to achieve those goals. So, if you're setting new goals in your business, talk about them as much as you can. Write about them. Use newsletters, posters, e-mails, rallies, bull sessions—anything to get people comfortable with them. A new level of articulation will build confidence that those goals are attainable, that they're right, and that they will be accomplished.

Positive Self-talk

A third and closely related technique is that of positive self-talk. Throughout the centuries, many philosophers and psychologists have come to realize the importance to all human beings of what we hear said about ourselves, both by others and by ourselves.

How carefully do we guard our exposure to negative people, worry-warts, naysayers, and pessimists? What we hear others say can affect us even when we're not consciously aware of the effect—even when we consciously dismiss what we've heard them say. That's why one old friend once told me that he never reads reviews of his books. Early on in his writing career, he realized that he enjoyed good reviews for days and then forgot them, whereas he could still quote the bad ones word for word years later.

Man is so made that by continually telling him
he is a fool he believes it, and by continually telling
it to himself he makes himself believe it.
For man holds an inward talk with himself alone,
which it behooves him to regulate well.
Blaise Pascal (1623–1662)

Whenever I'm planning a new project or deciding on some new goals, I try to solicit the advice and reactions of people whose wisdom, practical savvy, and gut instincts I admire, individuals who may be able to warn, inform, or encourage me in a well-positioned way. I know better than to consult any doom-and-gloomers. I can't afford the unnecessary negativity. And neither can you. If such a person is literally unavoidable on the feeding chain, manage your own reactions to the negativist as carefully as you can. Minimize what you hear, do what you can to consider the source, and then move forward.

Most important of all, though, is what you hear yourself saying to yourself. If you're up against a difficult challenge, the truly remarkable fact is that negative self-talk can lower the objective probability of your success, whereas positive self-talk can raise the objective likelihood that you'll do well.

The highest possible stage in moral culture is when
we recognize that we ought to control our thoughts.
Charles Darwin (1809–1882)

How we think about something, how we talk to ourselves about it in the quiet of our own minds, can boost or erode both our confidence in ourselves and our ability to draw on our talents and preparation at the highest possible level. We owe it to ourselves and those around us to govern our thoughts in such a way as to empower ourselves to the greatest extent possible for the good we're capable of doing.

How do you talk to yourself about new challenges? Do you ever give yourself little pep talks? You deserve it. And you need it, if you're like most people. But what if you consider yourself a little bit above hokey techniques of mental cheerleading? Maybe you think of yourself as just a little too intelligent to engage in stupid games of internal do-it-yourself brainwashing.

Remember, the smarter you are, the more you need positive self-talk to counter the naturally higher levels of anxiety highly intelligent people are prone to. So no one should think of themselves as exempt from the need for self-governance at the level of thought. We all can use an inner boost every now and then.

Don't even joke about yourself negatively on any regular basis. Other people may enjoy your self-deprecating putdowns, but your unconscious mind doesn't have such a good sense of humor. Even though the unconscious can make a joke, it can't easily take a joke. It absorbs everything with a surprising amount of literalness. It's vulnerable to negative humor, which unintentionally can erode both your felt confidence and your actual performance level.

Our whole duty is to think as we ought.
Blaise Pascal

I often use all the positive techniques of visualization, articulation, and self-talk before giving a public speech. I telephone my wife and tell her how nice the people are, how much I'm looking forward to the event, and how well it's going to go. I envision laughing people, intense interest, and a good time had by all. I physically smile while I'm doing this. If I'm alone, it can be a huge, almost painful grin, which releases positive brain chemicals in just the right way. In a hotel room, getting dressed, I'll run positive images through my head, look into a mirror, grin like a maniac, and say out loud, "This is going to be so great I can't believe it!" I sometimes say it a second time, laugh at myself, and then walk out of the room, ready for action.

But I have to admit that I've learned to be careful about where and how I do this. Recently, in a huge hotel, I received a phone call in my room about an hour earlier than I had planned on dressing and making my way down to the convention center for my speech. The meeting was running very early, so I had to get into my suit as quickly as possible and run down the hall to the elevator, and then through an enormous lobby over to the meeting area. Spotting a men's room as I hurried along, I ducked in for one last minute preparation. Apparently alone, I stepped into the first stall, mentally recalled that I had not yet done my confidence-building self-talk, and without thinking where I was said out loud, "This is going to be so great I can't believe it!" From two stalls down, a man loudly cleared his throat. I thought about explaining to him that I was just doing a little confidence building, but instead I decided just to let it drop and get out of there as quickly as possible.

Our personal confidence building with positive self-talk should be accomplished with as much privacy as we can find.

Competence Building

Visualizing, articulating, positive self-talk—these are all examples of inner psyching, the first of three distinct methods for building confidence toward achieving a specific goal. But you can't expect to hold anxiety at bay only by inner psyching.

It is folly to bolt the door with a boiled carrot.
English Proverb

The most basic method we have is this: To build confidence, build competence.

Nothing creates and undergirds a confident disposition like knowing you're prepared for the challenge. Nothing bolts the door against fear and worry like knowing you are competent. So for any new challenge, prepare yourself in advance as well as possible. Prepare your team as well as you can. And let them know how they stand in readiness. Give them the tools to get the job done and then make sure they understand how these tools will work.

The athletes who are most successful at using such techniques as visualization, articulation, and positive self-talk are those who have done the most work to hone their skills and raise their competence level; these are ultimately the fundamental tools of success. There is no way to short-circuit that process. Mental techniques can enhance, but can never replace, the hard work of preparation. Great confidence is rooted in great preparation. Only those who prepare for greatness can reasonably expect it.

Directed Action

In addition to inner psyching, and competence building, there is a third main path to the creation and maintenance of confidence: directed action. I like to call it "the Action Approach to Attitude."

The bravest thing you can do when you are not brave
is to profess courage and act accordingly.
Corra Harris (1869–1935)

Launch out in pursuit of your goal. Certain types of competence building and confidence building can happen only when we are under way and fighting our way forward.

The human mind is strange. It's uncomfortable with anything to which it hasn't been habituated. But it becomes habituated to something new with amazing ease. The water can look cold from the edge, and feel frigid when you poke in your toe. But once you jump in, it's wild how quickly you adjust.

How many times have you stood on the edge of a new opportunity or novel challenge, inwardly shivering at the sight. Maybe putting your toe into the situation makes it worse. Often, though, I bet if you jumped in, you found yourself acclimated in no time at all, swimming along with ease.

People wish to learn to swim and
at the same time to keep one foot on the ground.
Marcel Proust (1871–1922)

We are adaptable beings, created to flex and flourish amid extraordinary change. If you can trust this aspect of human nature as it is expressed in you, and trust yourself to a new situation that you've decided is right for you, you'll find *in via,* on the road, along the way, resources for confidence building unavailable to the timid bystander. So if it's right for you, take the leap and enjoy the ride. That is the real art of confidence building.

PART 3

THE ART OF CONCENTRATION

Art is the path of the creator to his work.

Ralph Waldo Emerson

CHAPTER

Concentrated Effort

CONDITION 3 OF THE 7 CS:

*We need a focused **Concentration** on what it takes to reach the goal.*

The best things are the most difficult.
Plutarch (ca. 46–126)

It's has been said that the only secret to success is hard work. I believe that this, like many catchy sayings, is an exaggeration wrapped around an insight.

We live in a culture whose obsession with external forms of success, involving primarily money and fame, is equaled only by its fixation on shortcuts to those goals. How-to-get-rich-quick schemes have multiplied as fast as instant diets in the past few decades. We're always looking for an easy way, for some little-known and quasi-magical formula that will practically do our work for us, while we spend our time just thinking about how we'll spend that money, enjoy that fame, and flaunt that new physique.

Following the advice of motivational gurus, people have mimicked the body language of millionaires, memorized the names of half the planet, practiced smiling in front of a mirror each morning, watched infomercials after midnight, and called those 800 numbers to order every money-back-guaranteed, one-time-only, special-price videotape series on success that there is. It seems like people will try almost anything that promises to help them get what they want right now.

There is no substitute for hard work.
Thomas Edison (1847–1931)

Many of us lose track of an insight articulated by wise people from Sophocles to Thomas Edison and beyond. There is no shortcut to satisfying success. There is no instant, magic elixir for real achievement.

But this shouldn't be viewed as disappointing at all. Success is satisfying only if it's the result of work we've actually done. There is no pride in winning a lottery. Excitement, sure. And anyone could enjoy spending the money. But the rewards of real success are deeper. And they are deeper primarily because they've been earned.

Nothing ever comes to one that is worth having,
except as a result of hard work.
Booker T. Washington (1856–1915)

THE PROCESS OF SUCCESS

The harder a job is, the more satisfying its successful completion can be. This is almost the simplest common sense imaginable, but it can ring strange to an ear attuned to the cadences of the modern world. Let's face it, we live in Lotto Land. Everybody wants to hit the jackpot.

We distinguish the excellent man from the common man by saying
that the former is the one who makes great demands on himself,
and the latter who makes no demands on himself.
Jose Ortega y Gassett (1883–1955)

Too many people dream of the results of success and ignore the process. Of course, a measure of this kind of thinking is only natural. When the results of success can be dramatic, beautiful, and exciting, it's easy to fantasize about them, to the extent that they begin to dominate our attention. Dazzled by the rewards we envision, we are blinded to the necessity of focused hard work for attaining those rewards.

Business owners who have been around for at least a few decades in the world of commerce often tell me that job interviews over the past several years with young people just out of college have been quite discouraging at times. The eager applicants ask not what they can do for the business, but what the business can do for them. Salary, benefits, vacation time, bonuses, travel, expense accounts—these are the objects of primary curiosity. "Do I get a car?" "How fast can I expect to get promoted?" There's nothing wrong with these questions, if they are not all that's on the applicant's mind. But what has come to be known as "the entitlement mentality" has gotten out of control in recent years.

Everywhere in life,
the true question is not what we gain,
but what we do.
Thomas Carlyle

The entertainment media certainly encourage an unrealistic attitude toward work. The most common images in movies and on television can create in younger viewers some seriously skewed expectations that life should always involve expensive products and the effusive admiration of others; problems that are solved within a couple of hours, usually with an attractive companion; and happy endings that emerge magically from unbelievably dramatic everyday happenings whirling all around. To put it mildly, this doesn't prepare people well for what real life most often requires. Of course, it's not intended to do so. But if a culture dominated by images of beautiful people doing exciting things with high-priced toys does not provide its young people with sufficiently counterbalancing images and realistic messages about life, success, and fulfillment, entertainment that would otherwise be harmless becomes a dangerous kind of teaching, and bad preparation for daily existence in the world.

The prizes of life are never to be had without trouble.
Horace (65–8 B.C.)

Life is the process more than the results. And the results don't have the value they're capable of having unless they are the product of a process of hard work. In addition, it's almost universally true that the results we want are not very likely to materialize without an arduous preparation process. We need to remember this in all our pursuits.

Hard work, if it is to be productive, must involve a perceptive and focused concentration on exactly what it will take for us to make progress toward our goals. Working hard at the wrong things won't ever get us the progress we want. There is an ancient art of concentration available to each of us that will help us to attain exactly the sort of focus that we need. Without a mastery of this art, all our efforts can misfire. So let's look at what it requires.

BIG DREAMS, SMALL DEEDS

If you wish to reach the highest, begin at the lowest.
Publilius Syrus

Losing sight of the importance of hard work is not just a problem for young people. Even in a business context we can easily forget the importance day to day of the sometimes tedious and difficult work we have to do to make the good things happen. Dreamers of big dreams have to learn to be doers of small deeds in order to position themselves to make their dreams come true. This is the first lesson in the art of focus.

A former colleague of mine at Notre Dame, the legendary college football coach Lou Holtz, tells an interesting story about his early years in the game. As a young man he was fired from a job as an assistant coach. With a family to support and no source of income, he could have been very depressed, and could have given up. But instead, he decided to sit down and write out some goals for his life. He was firmly convinced that he should aim high in his planning, so he began to write down goals like "One day, become the head coach at Notre Dame," "Win a national championship," "Appear on the *Tonight Show* with Johnny Carson," "Get invited to the White House," "Jump out of an airplane—with a parachute," "Get a hole-in-one in golf," and on and on. He ended up setting over one hundred exalted life goals for himself.

When he finished, he was bursting with pride. He would aim high, follow his dreams, and not settle for anything less. Greatness was the target. He eagerly took the list to show his wife. He says she looked it over quietly, read it all the way through, and then said the one thing he would least have expected her to say. She commented, "Lou, you left out something. Why don't you add 'Get a job'?"

Slight not what's near, though aiming at what's far.
Euripides

This is the challenge: to balance big plans with small details—never to allow the glow of our most exalted dreams to blind us to the sometimes duller everyday realities we need to attend to in pursuit of those visions. We get to what's far by attending to what's near. And this takes discipline, a neglected virtue in the modern world.

I believe that this sort of discipline, or self-discipline, can be understood in the same way Aristotle described virtues. Some people pride themselves on being "big picture thinkers." Others are proud of being "detail people," implementers with a precision mentality. It certainly is possible to go to an extreme in either direction. Many people do. Perhaps a balance that encompasses both emphases is really what's needed. Think of a spectrum of possible focus, with the wide-eyed visionaries and dreamers on one end and the carefully analytical, scrupulously precise people on the other. Don't we all, to the extent possible for us, need to embody a bifocal, composite mentality, representing a sort of midpoint balance?

Only this combination will allow us to chart any goal pursuit properly from the start, and then steer our way through the rapids we'll inevitably encounter on our voyage of success. We need to be both large-scale strategic thinkers and small-scale tacticians, always remembering that apparent importance and real importance are not often the same. Small steps can launch huge ventures. And little details can often be seen in retrospect to have had an immeasurably great impact on the attainment of any worthy goal.

We should always be thinking on two levels. We need to set goals and attend to process. The benefits of focusing on matters of process are of two kinds. First and foremost, a top-notch process—hard work and intelligent strategy directed toward a goal—makes a good outcome much more likely to occur. Good work most often has good results. But there is a second and more subtle point to be made.

If the building of a bridge does not enrich the awareness of those who work on it, then that bridge ought not to be built.

Frantz Fanon (1925–1961)

I've come to believe that we are here in this world to discover and develop talents that will contribute to the welfare of others as well as ourselves. Mother Teresa (1910–1997) was once asked how she can devote so much time and effort to helping people who are dying, knowing that those she has lavished her work on will in fact pass away. She replied by saying that we are called not to be successful but to be faithful. I think she was right to stress the need for faithfulness, but I also believe that this need not be separated from the best idea of success, when it is deeply understood.

The success we are here to have involves being able to participate in processes that bring out our talents and enrich our experience. We're here to make our contribution to the grand process every day, in often small ways and sometimes big ways. Some of us are called to ventures that will yield great wealth and recognition. Others will toil quietly in tasks unrewarded by the general culture but appreciated deeply by the people who matter to us most. Whenever an individual's talents have been discovered, developed, and used for the good of others, some measure of true success has been achieved.

To work is to pray.

St. Benedict of Nursia (ca. 480–ca. 543)

We are not all called to obviously dramatic, glamorous work, but we are all intended to engage in good work. Concentrated effort—plain old hard work—is what it takes to realize any difficult goal. And that is exactly what it takes to sculpt and polish a human life into the work of art it is intended to be.

One thing that I've learned many times is this: Everything worth doing is harder than it seems. I sometimes find that things are stunningly more difficult than I had anticipated. But that's all right. As long as we don't expect things to be easy, difficulty won't needlessly frustrate us. It need not cause us to suffer. On the contrary, difficulty often challenges us to be creative and persistent, to dig deep within our internal resources, to learn what we're made of, and to use all our intelligence to overcome the obstacles we face. Difficulty can ground us and expand us as nothing else does.

It is difficulties that show what men are.

Epictetus

Without challenge we don't develop, and without personal development, we never feel the deep satisfaction we're capable of experiencing. Difficulty draws us back to the importance of hard work, to the significance of good planning, and to the necessity of executing our plans to the best of our abilities. Part of the art of concentration is to be able to keep our heads, maintain our focus on our goals, and continue to work toward them when even the most daunting obstacles come to stand in our way.

I have learned this in deeply personal ways. About seventy-five minutes into what was scheduled to be a ninety-minute talk on success, my mouth went completely dry. Suddenly I felt very dizzy. A couple of seconds later I noticed that I could not turn my head at all. My neck was completely paralyzed. I kept talking. Four seconds more and I felt a sensation as though boiling liquid were being poured over my whole body. As you can imagine, this was a bit distracting. I was frantically trying to figure out what was happening as I outwardly kept my cool and continued speaking. Then I realized that I couldn't breathe. I tried to take a breath and my lungs would not work. My heart started pounding. I looked up at my audience and calmly said, "I can't breathe."

Fortunately, the one hundred or more people in my audience had all just been trained in CPR. Three gentlemen jumped on to the stage and quickly put me down on the floor. For about a minute, I thought I was dying. The physical jarring of hitting the floor started my lungs, but weakly. As they loosened my tie and removed my shoes, EMTs were instantly there. While putting me on the stretcher, one of them opened my shirt and exclaimed, "My God, I've never felt skin this hot!"—not exactly the most reassuring thing to hear at that moment. As they wheeled me out of the room, I suddenly realized that I had been struck down at the end of talking about the sixth condition of success. My audience had not heard the seventh. So as I was being wheeled out the door to the ambulance, in front of the stunned and silent crowd, I turned my head and said, as loudly as I could, "Number seven—a capacity to enjoy the process!"

Examine the lives of the best and most fruitful people and peoples and ask yourselves whether a tree that is supposed to grow to a proud height can dispense with bad weather and storms; whether misfortune and external resistance, some kinds of hatred, jealousy, stubbornness, mistrust, hardness, avarice, and violence do not belong among the favorable *conditions without which any great growth even of virtue is scarcely possible.*

Friedrich Nietzsche

Two visits to the emergency room and six weeks in bed later, with no clear diagnosis of what had happened, I finally thought I was over whatever the problem had been, and flew to Los Angeles for my next scheduled speech that hadn't been canceled. After the talk, which I had to do sitting, I was flat on my back in the hotel room with two doctors hovering over me. "Get to the Mayo Clinic as soon as possible," one of them said. "I don't know what's wrong with you, but it's neurological, and it's serious."

Three days later, a doctor at the Mayo Clinic told me I most likely had Ciguatera food poisoning from eating a tainted piece of grouper two days before my symptoms appeared. A meal at a five-star restaurant with my family had almost killed me, and had made my son so sick that he missed five weeks of school. The doctor said I would most likely have episodic symptoms of severe dizziness, overall weakness, limited amnesia, and extreme skin heat for up to five years, and that I was lucky to have lived through the onset of symptoms, as extreme as they had been. I should get as much rest as possible, and pace my travel for long term recovery.

The artist is extremely lucky who is presented with the worst possible ordeal which will not actually kill him. At that point, he's in business.

John Berryman (1914–1972)

A week later, I did something that my doctor had predicted would be impossible. I gave an energetic three-hour talk on ethics to hundreds of Chase Manhattan Bank managers. I had to steady myself with my hand on the side of a table to stand upright. They were completely unaware of my inner struggle to be able to speak at all. I did my job with all the enthusiasm I could muster and got a rousing ovation from people who didn't know anything about my condition but just appreciated the content of what I had given them, and the animated delivery, which came from deep in my heart.

I learned for the next two years what I was capable of doing, teaching classes at Notre Dame when I could barely stand up, yet doing it with all the passion I could muster. Flying to give talks around the country when my body ached to rest, I had to plan around my limitations to give my audiences the best of what I had to offer. And I needed to attain a new concentration of focus on the process.

In all those bouts of nearly debilitating symptoms, I learned in a very personal way the power of the human spirit to prevail. And I learned what it takes to hold on to your focus in times of struggle. I had met many other people over the years who had overcome much greater physical and mental ordeals, and I had benefited tremendously from the lessons that their lives and victories were able to offer me. But it was the firsthand experience of overcoming such hardship that really opened my eyes.

It's genuinely incredible what we're capable of handling. I didn't talk in public about the difficulties of those years while I was still going through them. But I found them to be an extremely fertile source of philosophical understanding. If we react in the right way, adversity can strengthen us tremendously. We can come to new depths of self-knowledge. We can see vividly what determination can accomplish, against the odds. And we can learn what hard work really is. By the end of five years, I was basically symptom-free. And I had come to believe that I can do almost anything.

We all have some form of greatness within us. And it's often the hard times that bring it out. Part of the art of concentration is to be able to maintain our proper direction during times of hardship and learn from our toughest experiences. Our troubles are our teachers. No problem that I've faced since the most intense days of my five-year struggle with Ciguatera has ever seemed overwhelming. Problems can detain us, and can reroute us in unexpected ways, but they can't stop us unless we let them.

A difficulty raiseth the spirits of a great man.

George Savile, marquis of Halifax (1633–1695)

In recent sports history, there is no story more informative and inspirational than that of the cyclist Lance Armstrong. A local and national champion in bicycle racing, he was suddenly struck down in his twenties with testicular cancer. Before it was diagnosed, the disease had spread throughout his body, including his lungs and brain. The prognosis was grim. But his attitude was extraordinary. His focus was intense. He tackled the problem of treatment as he would a major new race course. He researched the options and found the best experts. Then, together they formed a plan. He went on to suffer almost unimaginable agonies in chemotherapy, and struggled mightily to maintain his goals as dreams for the future. His body was wrecked. But he began to rebuild it. He floundered in focus. But with the help of his wife he recovered. He entered races once more, now against all odds, and he lost. But the worst thing in his life had prepared him for some of the best things imaginable, yet to come, in unexpected ways. Only work, patience, and persistence would be required.

Cancer and chemotherapy had reconfigured Lance Armstrong's body so that he was now anatomically and physiologically able to prepare for and compete in a different kind of race, an ultimate endurance event—in fact, the most difficult bicycle race in the world, the amazingly arduous 2,200-mile Tour de France of 1999. He worked harder to prepare than most people can even imagine. He lived the focused concentration that is our third condition of success and mastered the art of its use every day. And it all paid off, because the outcome of his amazingly arduous, focused work was the seemingly miraculous result that he not only finished the race but won.

A cancer survivor who was, in the eyes of the experts, lucky to be walking and talking at all had endured and won perhaps the most difficult athletic contest of any kind in the world. Through the art of concentration. And the hardest of work. And then he won it again. And yet once again, becoming the only American in history to win this grueling international contest an incredible three times in a row. Lance Armstrong's story is eloquent testimony to the strength of the human spirit to overcome apparently overwhelming adversity when we approach any situation with the full arsenal of our resources and a powerful determination to prevail.

The first prerogative of an artist in any medium
is to make a fool of himself.

Pauline Kael

Some of the greatest writers, the best musicians, the most pioneering scientists, and the most successful businesspeople in the world have been told early in the process that they should give up. They have faced rejection and repeated failure, obstacles they could not have anticipated, and hardships they found hard to believe. But they have endured. They have focused, worked, adjusted, strategized, and persisted almost to the point of looking ridiculous to many observers around them. And they have attained their own forms of personal greatness as a result.

It's ultimately up to us how we react to any external circumstance. Does a difficulty challenge us or defeat us? Do we inwardly smile at the vicissitudes of the adventure, or go into a downward spiral of despair and desperation? When things go outrageously wrong, I occasionally find myself laughing out loud. I've come to appreciate the sometimes absurdist humor in the unexpected hurdles we face along life's way. And I've come to realize that very little in this world is exactly what it at first seems to be. The blocked path can bring about great discoveries. The process is everything. Challenge is the door to growth. And concentrated effort is the key.

CHAPTER

Action Planning

9

The world is sown with good;
but unless I turn my glad thoughts into
practical living and till my own field,
I cannot reap a kernel of that good.
Helen Keller (1880–1968)

What will it take to reach your goals? Have you begun to focus on the process? Have you concentrated enough effort on planning? Have you taken the first steps in that direction, however small?

If not, what's holding you back?

If you have taken these steps, it's important that you plan as well as you can; then your actions will have maximum impact.

We can't always wait for others to act, or for circumstances to develop that are favorable to our goals. We need to be able to take charge of our own trajectory in pursuit of any new objective and make the changes that will move us in the direction we want to go. This is an important part of the art of concentration.

In this chapter, we'll consider two aspects of action planning: (1) the creative task of charting out our actions in pursuit of a goal, and (2) the vital role of initiative in taking action with those plans.

To will is to select a goal,
determine a course of action that will bring one to that goal,
and then hold to that action 'til the goal is reached.
The key is action.
Michael Hanson (1863–1908)

To adopt a goal is itself to begin to take action in a new direction with a specific, clear end in view. Action is the key. If you're not moving in a new way, you haven't really set yourself a new goal. It's just that simple. It's one thing to be thinking about adopting a new goal. It's another to have actually embraced a new goal as your own. Having a goal involves acting differently. And acting intelligently involves having an action plan.

In this dynamic, complex world, no one sets up a worthwhile, challenging target and simply hits it with effortless ease. We have to anticipate what it will take to get the job done, decide where our best efforts need to be directed, and prepare for all reasonably foreseeable contingencies along the way.

MAPPING OUR GOALS

Archery is an ancient model for the art of concentration. To hit a target, an archer needs to know more than where the target is. She needs to know where she is relative to the target, and what she has to do to get the arrow from her bow to the bull's-eye. She must be aware of any obstacles that could stand in her arrow's way. Does the distance mean she has to shoot higher than the target? Do prevailing winds require a compensating aim? Will the target move between release and strike time? All these things need to be understood. Then she can lock in on the process most likely to lead her to her goal.

Everything in this world is a moving target. That's why we need to gather information as completely as we can, and update it as much and as often as we can. Any process of achieving a challenging success is an ongoing enterprise of concentrated learning. And the most effective application of whatever we do learn requires intense focus.

Our example here is telling. Archery isn't just a sport. It's an art. The process of hitting any difficult target requires skill. No one can do it for us, but we can learn in outline from those who have gone before us and who have done it well. Then we must discipline ourselves to apply what we've learned.

The man who would emancipate art from discipline
and reason is trying to exclude rationality,
not merely in art, but in all existence.
George Santayana (1863–1952)

Drawing Our Map

Art requires logic. There is a deep rationality to productive creativity, despite what many bohemian artists may have said to the contrary. There are universal structures within which any positive action takes place in this world. This doesn't detract at all from the originality of our endeavors. It's rather what makes creative work possible. There is, in particular, a logical structure to action planning that is essential to the art of concentration, and it needs to be grasped clearly in any process of personal or organizational achievement.

The logic of action planning is basically very simple. In any new enterprise, we need as a first step a three-fold map to orient us and give us direction.

The Three-fold Map

In any new endeavor, we first need to do three things:

1. Understand our actual starting point.
2. Define our ideal end-state.
3. Identify a primary path from here to there.

It is interesting to note that this is perfectly congruent with the fundamental structure of all the world's great religious traditions. In Christianity, Judaism, Islam, Hinduism, Buddhism, and every other major religion, we are given a three-fold map: a diagnosis of the human condition, a conception of the ideal human state of being, and a path of salvation to follow to get from one to the other. The religious mapping can be understood simply as laying out these three things:

1. The Problem
2. The Ideal
3. The Path from the Problem to the Ideal

Mapping with this scheme can be done by any of us.

A traveler without knowledge is a bird without wings.

Mosharref Sa'di, Persian classical poet (ca. 1213–1292)

We can begin our pursuit of any new goal most effectively by first asking just three simple questions:

1. *The Problem: Where are we now?*

Examples of answers could look like this:

At the office: We may have high expenses, or low customer retention. We may be losing good people.

In personal matters: I may be overweight, I may not be with my children enough. Perhaps I need to make more money.

2. *The Ideal: Where do we want to be?*

Examples of answers may be:

At the office: We may decide we need a few strategic partnerships. We may want to increase repeat business by 25 percent. Our people need to feel they're appreciated, and growing.

In personal matters: I need to lose twenty pounds. I realize I should be reading aloud to my children nightly. I may decide that I need to increase my annual income by at least 30 percent.

3. *The Path: How can we get there?*

Examples of answers here might be:

At the office: We should begin researching potential business partners. Perhaps we should initiate new educational and rewards programs to show our people how much we value them. To increase repeat business, we may assign accounts to teams who will work with customers collaboratively.

In personal matters: I may commit myself to an hour of fast walking each day and weightlifting three days a week. I may take my children shopping for some books I could read them at bedtime, and set aside the half hour before they go to sleep to do so. I may work on an income-generating hobby.

Plans get you into things,
but you got to work your way out.
Will Rogers (1879–1935)

Of course, simple identifications like these are only a beginning. Lots of details need to be filled in. But the basic map work gives us a grid for spelling out more specifics while at the same time keeping an overall perspective on the plan we're creating. Every new detail will be an elaboration of the problem, or of the ideal, or of the path between the two.

The more difficult the problem we're facing, the more challenging the goal, the more important a preliminary mapping will be, and the more crucial it will be to fill in our map with lots of details. We often find that the harder we plan, the easier we work.

Many things difficult to design prove easy to performance.
Samuel Johnson (1709–1784)

ANTICIPATING DIFFICULTIES

The path we chart is our action plan. It's vital that in preparing for any new enterprise, we anticipate difficulties that may arise along the way. What obstacles could we face? What could go wrong? By thinking through all the possible obstacles, we position ourselves to prepare contingency solutions and backup plans we can adapt to whatever situations we face along the way.

Such preparation is necessary because if there is one guarantee in this world, it's that we'll confront numerous problems in our pursuit of any worthwhile aim. But that's all right. Problems are just life's way of getting the best out of us. They make us creative. They enforce patience, and create the conditions under which we build fortitude and persistence, important strengths of character for any life of success. Problems teach us and develop us, even when they irritate us beyond belief.

Problems are only opportunities in work clothes.
Henry J. Kaiser (1882–1967)

FLEXIBILITY

The best planning is always flexible. We should be ready to respond to problems as well as to more obvious opportunities with new moves that might not have been a part of our original plan. The third universal condition of success, a focused concentration on what it will take to reach our goal, means to enjoin an ongoing concentration sensitive to shifting conditions, developing possibilities, and moving targets.

Inflexible plans tie us down. A common failing in business and life is an inability to adapt to change. This is sometimes due to a fear of looking uncertain, as if change is always vacillation. But nothing is a better sign of intelligence than the ability to adapt quickly to meet unforeseen contingencies. Proper concentration always involves a flexible firmness in pursuing our goals.

PLAN IMPLEMENTATION AND ADJUSTMENT

When we first start our planning, we make a simple three-fold map. But then we begin to fill in the details. Do I have a friend or colleague with talents that could help in this challenge? Is there someone I've never worked with who might contribute? Do we need to bring in advisers at this preliminary stage? What research could be of use?

I also need to consider whether I'm ready for setbacks along the way. Am I prepared to turn apparent defeat into eventual victory? Do I have the flexibility of mind to change my plans if developments demand it? Will I listen if someone comes to me with what may be a better idea than the one I'm already using?

Every man takes the limits of his own
field of vision for the limits of the world.
Arthur Schopenhauer (1788–1860)

Should we plan as a team? Everyone's experience is limited. We all have different talents and histories. We view the world through different lenses. If I don't have the input of others, I'm likely to miss some important details in my planning projections. Creativity often requires solitude, but at other times it loves a crowd. When we work with others in the early stages of planning, we act as mutual correctives to each other's blind spots. The best attainments often result from a healthy dose of collaborative insight.

So, alone or in partnership with others, we begin to inventory our resources and map out a plan to our objective. When we have enough of a plan to act on, the next step is, quite simply, to take action on it. We can't allow our concern for planning—indispensable as it is—to become a substitute for acting, for taking the initiative and launching out into our new venture. Despite all the virtues of planning, if it's not controlled properly, it can lead to an endless process of postponed action.

He who considers too much will perform little.
J. C. F. von Schiller (1759–1805)

I can speak here from personal experience. It's a philosopher's job to sit and think. We like to consider and reflect, checking, analyzing, and reconsidering before we move to any conclusions, lest we leap rashly beyond a justifiable inference. But there is a time when the thinker must become a doer. We come to a point where we have to trust our instincts and move forward.

Away with delay!
The chance of great fortune is short-lived.
Silius Italicus (ca. 25–101)

TAKING ACTION

We usually don't recognize a new problem as such until the time has come for a change. What has brought the problem to our attention in the first place is actually the building up of forces that will facilitate change. These forces also imply a new ideal, and the need for a path of action to take us there. The chance lies waiting to be taken, but it will not often wait for long. If we do not act when the stage is set, we risk losing the momentum of those forces that have brought us into the process of planning. At that point, without action, we're in danger of losing our opportunity for maximally effective change.

There is danger in delay.
Livy (ca. 59 B.C.–17 A.D.)

We want to do our best in planning for any new goal, but it is not necessary to have a perfect plan before we can act. In fact, the planning process should not stop when you start to take action. Planning at its best is never complete until the goal is reached. Even then, as we'll see, new planning should begin.

Taking action is an important step in the planning process for at least two different reasons. One is generally epistemological—having to do with the details of how we know—and the other is metaphysical—having to do with the deep structure of what there is. Let's take a quick look at these two reasons for the importance of action. First, a point of general epistemological reflection:

No one ever drew up his plans for life so well
but what the facts, and the years,
and experience always introduce some modification.
Terence

Action Epistemology

Philosophically speaking, epistemology is the study of knowledge and belief. One of the most fundamental epistemological truths is that knowledge comes from action and experience. A rolling stone may gather no moss—whatever that means—but a rolling stone with a brain and perceptual capacities could in principle gather lots of information as it bounces along its way.

There is an important reason why the best plans most often are flexible ones. We can never know as much at the beginning of a journey as we'll learn along the way. Our initial map is meant to get us going in the right direction either to hit the target, or else to gather the information we'll need for getting there.

Upfront knowledge in any endeavor is necessarily incomplete. We need action to open up to us the knowledge that will otherwise be unavailable. We can never see what's on the other side of the next high hill until we walk around it, or climb to its peak. This is the point of general epistemology that we need to understand.

What we have to learn to do, we learn by doing.
Aristotle

Metaphysical Luck

Properly directed action is metaphysically advantageous. Tell that to a friend and see how they react. But then be prepared to explain. Metaphysics is the most fundamental philosophical account of the underlying nature of all existence. It is a basic metaphysical observation that chance, luck, or randomness often seem to be part of the underlying dynamism of our world. Randomness is, by definition, not completely predictable. We're all well advised to expect the unexpected in life, and yet it is impossible to know exactly what unexpected thing to expect! We can just remain open for unexpected opportunities, and be ready to take advantage of them. Luck never produces success, but it can produce unplanned opportunities for success. Only when we take action can we put opportunity to use.

I never did anything worth doing by accident;
nor did any of my inventions come by accident;
they came by work.
Thomas Edison

If we're well prepared to move toward our goal and take a flexible attitude about how to get there, if we hone our abilities and work our hardest with the best upfront plan we can develop, we'll be out there in the world, moving along, meeting people and seeing things we would not otherwise have seen. We'll be giving luck a big target, and we'll be well prepared to make the most of any fortuitous opportunity that comes our way, however unexpected.

Work lays the foundations for discovery, and paves the way to our goals. Without moving into the world and working with our plans, we never position ourselves to come across the lucky breaks life is prepared to toss into our path. It takes action to benefit from chance. And then, of course, a properly flexible plan will be adapted to make the most of what chance has provided. This will, necessarily, be a twist or turn that could not have been predicted or planned initially. You can't chart every note of a great jazz performance in advance. And you can't script a successful adventure in detail.

LEARNING FROM FAILURE

There is one more reason planning should give way to action sooner rather than later. It allows us to get any initial mistakes and failures out of our way more quickly. We should include within our plans the strong likelihood that there will be some misfires and temporary disappointments along the way, since this is just a universal aspect of any learning curve. If we expect mistakes, we aren't so jolted when they happen. And the sooner we experience them, the faster we can learn.

Anything worth doing is worth doing badly. At first. In order to learn. We learn by doing, and we succeed by overcoming. No challenging enterprise will be without its setbacks and detours. The sooner we confront this inevitable feature of everything worthwhile, the better we're equipped for real-world success. The ability to counter a reversal of fortune is an important skill within the art of concentration. Every beautiful tapestry has its knobby underside. Every success is built on failure.

The greatest test of courage on earth
is to bear defeat without losing heart.
R. G. Ingersoll (1833–1899)

Expect disappointment. And prepare to dismiss it. If we can diminish the negative emotions inevitably associated with any disappointment and maximize the experiential learning it makes possible, we position ourselves to move forward the most effectively toward our ultimate goals. The better we understand the necessary role of disappointment in the learning curve, the more easily we can minimize its intensity and duration when it comes.

Bearing defeat without losing heart becomes easier when we realize that failures can be the greatest learning experiences, positioning and empowering us for victory. Nietzsche famously said, "What does not kill me makes me stronger." We learn the most from the most difficult situations. And most difficult of all are the failures and defeats that we face. They are frustrating, sometimes frightening, and often embarrassing. But they are inevitable. And they can be used.

Wise people like to end each day with the question: "What have I learned today?" On days full of irritation, setbacks, and apparent failures, that simple question can magically turn negatives into positives. It can have a truly transformative impact.

Do not go to bed until you have
gone over the day three times in your mind.
What wrong did I do?
What good did I accomplish?
What did I forget to do?
Pythagorus (sixth century B.C.)

In the early stages of my work as a public philosopher, I once went through an unbelievably frustrating day of repeated disappointment. By the evening I was a mess of confusion and aggravation. But then I asked myself the question "What have I learned today?" A little calm reflection on the events that had transpired was a tremendous education, and gave me some exciting new perspectives. I learned to think of defeat as an educational experience that prepares and strengthens us for the future.

The ancient Stoics were right to stress the role of attitude in life. It doesn't matter so much what happens to us as how we think about what happens to us. If we use the bad as well as the good, we can often turn the bad into good.

No fine work can be done without concentration
and self-sacrifice and toil and doubt.
Max Beerbohm (1872–1956)

Of course, difficulties always generate a measure of self-doubt. And that can be perfectly healthy. Sometimes we need to rethink the specifics of our strategy. But that should never undermine our resolve to continue to work toward a proper objective. To deal with difficulty, we need a focused concentration, a willingness to sacrifice, and a capacity to work on toward the goal.

CHAPTER

Failure and Creative Triumph

Whatever you do,
do with all your might.
Cicero

Once there was an energetic young philosopher who wrote a book about satisfying success in life. Okay—it was me. And the book, *True Success*, was my first general-interest title, after a good number of volumes penned only for the scholarly "profundity" market, a sadly small niche of the book-buying public.

I went on my first book tour. This was something new. There had been no book tours for my scholarly books. The forty-seven people who will ever read those tomes know how to find them. But this was different. I was now doing philosophy for everybody, and my new publisher and I wanted everybody to know.

DISAPPOINTMENT AND CREATIVITY

The publisher attempted to get me on network television to promote my new book. No luck. The pitch was a little off. They actually said I could be "the Hegel of daytime TV." It was a bit unfortunate to be compared to the notoriously pedantic German idealist philosopher who wrote some of the world's most prolix academic prose two hundred years ago. "Next up, 'Disquisitions on the Absolute,' but first a word from our sponsor." Invitations were not exactly rolling in.

They tried to get me on my favorite midmorning show, *Live! With Regis and Kathie Lee,* which was then at a peak of its popularity, but they failed. The publicist told me their producer had said, "We don't do serious books. They don't work." Case closed.

I wanted to share some wisdom with Regis and Kathie Lee and, through them, with a lot more people. I figured that America needs a little good-morning philosophy every now and then. The publisher assured me it wouldn't happen. I should give up and move on.

This was bad advice. Somebody in the publicity department hadn't read the book. Or they weren't using what they had read. You don't give up on the basis of one defeat. That would be a strange policy for anyone to follow, but unfortunately, I think a lot of people do follow it. I couldn't. It takes a bit of courage to persist when you've been knocked down. But what's the alternative? Staying down?

That's courage—to take hard knocks
like a man when occasion calls.
Plautus (ca. 250–184 B.C.)

Let me give you a little more background. When I had a first draft of my book completed and was ready to get a publisher, I decided to send it to everyone I knew and respected who was connected to the world of the mass media. I had met Regis Philbin at a Notre Dame football practice and had seen him again at a party in South Bend. I was impressed with his humility in a real-life setting, and with the measure of practical wisdom he seemed to embody in conversation, so I sent him a copy of the manuscript. He liked it and gave me a rave review to forward to publishers. He even said, "Let me know when it comes out and we'll have you on the show."

So when the book was about to come out, the publicist for my publisher called the show and spoke to a producer. And she was turned down cold. She replied, "But Regis knows the author and wants him on the show." She was told: "Regis doesn't book the show. Thank you for calling." *Click.*

The most gifted members of the human species
are at their creative best when they cannot have their way.
Eric Hoffer

I didn't want to make a pest of myself, but I was not about to give up, either. So when I went on my book tour, I started sending Regis "Postcards From the Road" each day, with cartoons of me in front of bookstore audiences and short, funny notes about how I was getting ready for his show. There was no response to the cards. But then how many cards and letters came in each week addressed to Regis Philbin? Most likely the postcards weren't getting to him. I still was determined not to quit, as my publicist had. But how far do you go before you change strategy?

I decided at this point to push the creativity envelope and attempt to do one very creative thing before even considering the possibility of moving on. I needed to get my man's attention. I needed a plan that somehow would use both humor and insight.

We were now at a point a couple of months after the publication of my book, and most talk shows book authors for appearances only the week their book is out. Anything later makes it old news. So I had a new challenge. What could my hook be? It was early summer. Hey, why not "Success for Kids Going Back to School"? Success in college, success in high school. For over a decade I had taught as much as an eighth of the entire Notre Dame student body in some years. I knew what it took for kids to succeed in the classroom. A national association had even named me "Indiana Professor of the Year." Maybe I could use this as leverage. The publicist hadn't considered any such strategy at all.

A single idea, if it is right,
saves us the labor of an infinity of experiences.
Jacques Maritain (1882–1973)

So I went out to my local art-supply store and bought a four-foot-high plastic blow-up doll of a distraught man contorted in a scream, adapted from a famous expressionist painting by Edvard Munch called *The Scream.* I made a brightly colored cardboard sign to hang around its neck that said, "Why is this man in anguish? Because he's not yet seen Tom Morris on *Live! With Regis and Kathie Lee,* talking about success for kids going back to school." I had a friend in New York blow up the doll and deliver it, along with its sign, to Regis's apartment building in Manhattan, with assurances to the doorman that I was an old friend at Notre Dame.

Two days later I had a voice-mail message: "Tom, this is Regis Philbin. We'd like to have you on the show during Back-to-School Week in August to talk about how kids can have success at school, and what parents can do to help. Call my producer, Michael Gellman, and he'll set up everything." True success. A persistence of attitude and a plan with a little creativity can go a long way—if you play from your strength.

They had me on the show for six minutes, and the stars played with the book on camera for what seemed like forever. Regis said to the audience, "Get this book. It'll change your life!" and they put more copies of *True Success* in the hands of readers that day than everything else I did during the rest of my book tour combined. To top it all off, I had a great time. Both Regis and Kathie Lee were good fun. I came away with a strong impression of them as kind and gracious people who genuinely care about others and who worked hard to see to it that I was comfortable and had a good time on the show.

It was a success well worth attaining. And it came after apparent defeat. Repeated defeat. And disappointment. Rather than giving up, I developed Plan B. And then Plan C. And it worked.

Nothing in life just happens. You have to have the stamina to meet the obstacles and overcome them.

Golda Meir (1898–1978)

OPPORTUNISTIC ACTION PLANNING

Another account of initial discouragement and creative response will give us a deeper perspective on the art of concentrated and flexibly focused action in the world. It's a paradigmatic case of adaptive planning. And it shows how the right attitude can prevail when combined with creativity and initiative.

A friend from church, Joe Christian (yes, that's his actual name), had worked for many years as a stock broker. In early midlife he felt he needed a break. Something different. He hankered for a new adventure. So, in an act of midlife-crisis bravery, or foolhardiness, he quit his job and decided to experience something new. He read in the local paper that the Coen brothers were bringing a movie production to Wilmington, North Carolina, and that it was expected to be the next big blockbuster film. As a long-time fan of the Coens, he decided he'd go out to the movie studio and apply for a job.

The first day the film company set up its production office in town, Joe showed up at ten in the morning. He introduced himself to the one person there, explained that he had been a stock broker in the area, but now wanted to work in the movies, and that he had decided on coming to work for the Coen brothers on their new film. The lady behind the desk told him courteously that there were no jobs to be filled, and thanked him for dropping by. Joe pleasantly responded that he was sure something would develop, and that, when it did, he would be eager to get to work. She firmly reassured him that this would not be the case, and thanked him again for his interest. He said "Okay, I'll see you tomorrow," smiled, and left.

A man's wisdom gives him patience.
Proverbs 19:11

At ten the next morning, Joe walked into the office again, said good morning, and restated his eagerness to help with the movie. Once again he was assured that there were no jobs yet to be filled. The coordinator emphasized her complete confidence and sincerity in conveying this unwelcome news, reiterated her settled conviction that the situation would not change, and thanked him once more for his interest. He again left with a smile, determined to persist.

The next day at ten, he again showed up, ready for work. The same basic conversation ensued. But this time, there were other people around, in an adjoining room. The production staff had begun to arrive. As Joe visited with the now long-suffering coordinator, he overheard an animated conversation in the next room over what the good restaurants in the area might be. Expressing his heartfelt thanks once again for the opportunity to be considered for anything that might materialize, Joe left and drove straight to his ten favorite restaurants in town, requesting copies of their regular and take-out menus. When he got home, he went through the menus, annotating in his own hand the best dishes, and any other notes that might be helpful, took them all to be laminated, and put them in a three-ring binder, with his name and phone number prominently displayed.

The next morning, at his customary time, he arrived at the film office to deliver "The Joe Christian Guide to Wilmington Area Restaurants." Explaining that he had overheard some of the crew the previous day wondering about where to eat, he offered the notebook as something that might give them guidance, and once again voiced his enthusiasm about helping in any way with the production.

Never is work without reward,
or reward without work.
Livy

That night, Joe received a phone call at home from the director, newly in town, thanking him for the restaurant guide. No one had ever done such a thing. The director then asked Joe if he knew anything about real estate in the area. Joe, actually knowing no more about real estate than, well, the average Joe, confidently replied that he could provide any information that might be needed. The director then explained that he worried about local real estate people possibly having two price lists, one for regular folks and another for Hollywood types. He needed to house seventy-five people for the time they'd be in town for the production, and was concerned about staying within a reasonable budget for the rentals. As if he had done this all his life, Joe asked for an itemized list of exactly what they needed, took it around to local Realtors the next day, informed all of them that it would be a competitive situation and, as a result, successfully lined up suitably affordable places for the entire cast and crew within three days.

Whenever we do what we can,
we immediately can do more.
James Freeman Clarke (1810–1888)

Joe was then asked whether he might be interested in doing some of the driving for various cast and crew members to get to and from the set each day. He acted as though it was his greatest dream to be of such service to the film. One day early on, while driving the producer and engaging in small talk, this executive asked Joe what he knew about paint. The producer explained that the best set designer in Hollywood was soon to arrive, and was going to need a paint shop staffed with local painters to work on sets and props. Mentally reviewing the fact that he knew almost nothing about paint and local painters, Joe nonetheless told the producer that he would be glad to set up and run the paint shop for the production himself, seeing to it that all the right local people were involved. As a result, he was told to show up at the studio for a meeting the next Tuesday morning when the set designer would arrive on-site. He was also warned that this individual could be extremely demanding, and very difficult to work with.

Joe arrived just in time to see his potential employer walk in. "Who the hell are you?" was the greeting he received. Joe answered, "I'm the head of your new paint shop."

"What do you know about painting?" The question was blurted out with a belligerent glare.

"Well," Joe considered, "I once tried to paint a closet myself, got half done, gave up and decided to hire a professional painter to finish the job."

This was met with an incredulous stare. Joe continued, "But if you'll tell me what to do, I'll do it, and I'll run the best paint shop you've ever had." Apparently overwhelmed with the improbability and chutzpah of all this, the world-famous designer started barking orders to his eager new associate.

Each day, Joe had to come to work at five in the morning and stay until late at night. He learned as much as he could about paint, hired the right people, and found himself being asked for his opinion about colors by winners of Academy Awards. For all this effort, he worked his way up to earning fifty dollars a day. But he had the time of his life participating in a project staring Tim Robbins, Paul Newman, and a great supporting cast. The movie that resulted, and that was supposed to rack up awards while breaking box office records, was *The Hudsucker Proxy.* Joe took his fiancée to its local opening. And they enjoyed it tremendously with the three other people present. I've actually seen it too. On home video. Joe's paint looked great.

The highest reward for man's toil is not
what he gets for it but what he becomes by it.
John Ruskin (1819–1900)

This was Joe Christian's excellent adventure. So he didn't in the end make cinematic history. But he experienced, and he learned. Being persistent, flexible, opportunistic, and innovative got him beyond the gatekeepers, and into the midst of his dream. He had a goal. He acted with confidence. He refused to give up. And he adapted his planning as circumstances allowed. He displayed the ancient art of concentration in action. Joe was willing to start small. And in the end that led to the possibility of something big.

When the set designer was ready to leave town, he called Joe aside, praised his work to the highest, and invited him to come along to the next project, where, he promised, he could pay him some real money for running the paint shop and working on the sets. But my friend asked about what the project was, considered the proposal, and finally declined the opportunity, deciding to limit his movie career to one film. His big-screen reputation would have to rest on *Hudsucker.*

Joe recalls saying to himself, while considering the new job invitation, "*Forrest Gump*? No. Who's going to go see a movie called *Forrest Gump*?"

The man who makes no mistakes
does not usually make anything.
Bishop W. C. Magee (1821–1891)

Later realizing that his financial judgment was markedly superior to his cinematic insight, Joe started up his own business as an independent financial adviser, and in a very short time was doing better than ever, steering by his own values. The adventures in movie making had not at all been a dead end, but rather a refreshing detour that had allowed him to rethink his old business and eventually return reenergized to the work where his greatest talents lie.

A CONCLUDING THOUGHT

Each of us should ask regularly whether what we're doing is contributing to our happiness and the happiness of those around us. Are we aiming at the right goals, and are we pursuing them in the best way? Are we fulfilled by what we're doing? Do our families feel good about our activities, or are they in any way hurt by them? Are we learning? Do we feel energized by our goals and daily endeavors, or drained? Are we taking the initiative to make any changes that need to be made, and launching new activities that might lead us closer to the attainment of our goals?

Every day counts. The third of the seven universal conditions of success is that we need a focused concentration on what it takes to reach our goals. We need to be planners, learners, and doers, engaging in adaptive, focused thinking every day. That's how we best deploy our energies in the world, and it's how we experience the best that each stage of life has to offer.

Remember this, that very little is needed to make a happy life.
Marcus Aurelius (121–80 B.C.)

Any quest for a new form of achievement by its very nature produces some measure of anxiety. But we can master that emotional energy and direct it in such a way as to experience some measure of happiness in almost any circumstances as we move forward in pursuit of our goals. Creativity, opportunistic innovation, and habits of flexible planning can turn daunting challenges into enjoyable opportunities for personal growth. They are the component practices belonging to the art of focused concentration.

Deep personal happiness need not be held hostage by the vicissitudes of large-scale worldly success. Emperor Marcus Aurelius of Rome was right. Little accomplishments in our inner life of attitudes, plans, and initiatives manifested in various ways in the outer world can suffice for that measure of satisfaction or fulfillment we all want to feel in our ongoing experience of life achievement.

Happiness should not be an elusive quarry as we move forward in any proper quest for success. But it won't just take care of itself. We need to explore regularly how we can better refine the use of our time and energy so that our efforts result in greater happiness for those we love, as well as for ourselves. Great planning should always serve great goals. And this is among the greatest of them all.

PART 4

THE ART OF CONSISTENCY

Life is very nice, but it lacks form.
It's the aim of art to give it some.

Jean Anouilh (1910–1987)

CHAPTER

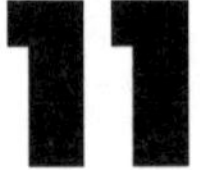

The Importance of Consistency

CONDITION 4 OF THE 7 CS:

*We need stubborn **Consistency** in pursuing our vision.*

Looking back, my life seems like one long obstacle race, with me as its chief obstacle.

Jack Paar (b. 1918)

In everything I write, I try always to be honest. I'll admit upfront that condition 4 is my own weakest area. This is the one condition of success I have the most trouble with, the one rule about effective goal pursuit I'm most likely to violate. Not with every kind of goal, but with some. It truly amazes me how often, in the process of shooting for a certain target, somewhere along the way I find myself acting as though I really intend to go in the opposite direction. I have struggled many times with the art of consistency.

If you had seen my dinner last night, you'd never guess what one of my personal goals is. You might speculate that I'm bulking up for a film role as a professional wrestler, but you'd not likely infer that I'm intent on losing ten pounds. I won't detail the menu. I'm sure you get the picture.

Why do we do this? Why do we ever act as the main obstacle to our own achievement? It's a common problem for creative people. Earlier, I made the point that a goal is a commitment of the will. Even strong commitments sometimes allow for occasional lapses. A momentarily stronger temptation comes along. We forget our resolve. We engage in a little self-deception razzle-dazzle. The concreteness of the moment overwhelms the relative abstractness of our intent. The spirit is willing, we say, but the flesh is weak.

Blessed is he who has never been tempted; for he knows not the frailty of his rectitude.

Christopher Morley (1890–1957)

HAVE YOU REALLY SET YOUR GOAL?

Here's a rarely noticed point that is well worth making. If your lapses from what you think you should be doing are fairly regular, this fact is a good indication that you haven't really set yourself the goal you think you have. The more exalted or remote from your present condition a goal is, the more it requires a commitment of the will to a process, an ongoing effort or pattern of effort. If you don't see in yourself any such positive pattern, then most likely you don't yet actually have the goal you think you have.

In case you're a little too clever for your own good, you might say to yourself at this juncture, "Fine. Then I can't possibly be responsible for ever failing because of inconsistency. If I act inconsistently enough to make it unlikely that a purported goal will be reached, then that is probably inconsistent enough to show that I didn't really have it as a goal in the first place, and it's impossible to fail with respect to a goal I don't have."

Think again. If you're that inconsistent, it shows you didn't even succeed at setting yourself the goal you thought you had, and if that's not failure of the first order, I don't know what is. You obviously lose the race when you can't even get out of the starting gate. Inconsistency is about the least likely thing around for saving us from failure. It is, on the contrary, one of the most pervasive causes of failure in the world today.

The word "consistent" derives its meaning from the Latin for "standing together." Do your actions and words stand together? Do your emotions, attitudes, and beliefs stand together? How about the members of your team, or office? Do they stand together with one vision, consistently working toward the same goals? What about your family? Are you all standing together, or are you pulling in different directions? Without consistency, things fall apart. Inconsistent behavior means that we are acting at cross purposes to ourselves and to each other.

The person who makes a success of living is the one who sees his goal steadily and aims for it unswervingly.

Cecil B. DeMille (1881–1959)

THE FORCE OF HABIT

Why would anyone ever act inconsistently in relation to his or her own goals and values? Why would anyone do anything self-defeating? On the surface, inconsistency can seem to be a form of behavior hard to explain. But the short answer to our questions is actually quite simple: temptation.

I can resist everything except temptation.
Oscar Wilde

Inconsistency most commonly enters a person's life through the doorway of temptation. And temptation operates by means of various forces that impinge on us from within and from without. Stress, pressure, distraction, laziness, fear, and passing urges all conspire to present us with situations in which we are tempted to turn aside from our fundamental principles, our basic values, and our chosen goals, and act out of character, drawn in that direction by the superficially attractive promise of short-term relief, pleasure, safety, status, financial gain, or comfort.

Within an individual's life, inconsistent behavior most commonly gets a foothold with significant help from the mechanism of self-deception. We lie to ourselves about a certain action's being consistent with our plans or values. Or we admit it's inconsistent, but deceive ourselves about its making a difference. "Just this once won't hurt anything," we whisper in our innermost souls. "It won't really matter." "I won't ever do it again, but this time is different."

Lying to ourselves is more deeply ingrained than lying to others.
Fyodor Dostoyevsky (1821–1881)

There are at least three problems with self-deceptive rationalizations. The first is that, whenever we lie to ourselves about anything, we loosen our grasp on reality, which erodes our ability to perceive and discern with clear-sightedness. And this is a capacity crucial for any form of sustainably successful living. The self-deceived person is not prepared to deal with reality.

Second, whenever we tell ourselves that some action we're contemplating which will violate our own commitments won't really matter, we're always going to be wrong. Everything matters. There are no actions small enough not to make a difference. Any beliefs we entertain to the contrary are not only false, but dangerous.

The third problem is that whenever we make any sort of exception for a "special" occasion, we make it just a little more likely that we will make the same exception again, despite any possible self-protestations and self-assurances to the contrary. Every action has repercussions in the actor. There are no exceptions to this rule. Whenever actions are performed, tendencies are planted or reinforced. Then they are nurtured until they grow full blown into habits. And habit is one of the strongest powers in human life.

Life is but a tissue of habits.
Henri Frédéric Amiel

Quite plausibly, life itself is dependent on the deep and stubborn entrenchment of habit. Without powerful habit formation, daily living would be far too complicated and real learning would never fully get into our bones. What would it be like if every morning you had to decide whether to put on your left or your right sock first? How could we live if we had to deliberate about every motion we make each day? Habits free our minds for facing the real challenges that come our way.

A positive habit can be a wonderfully potent force for good, allowing us to operate efficiently in known circumstances while we focus our conscious attention and decision-making skills on any unanticipated new developments that we might face. A bad habit, by contrast, can tie our hands and shackle our feet with surprising strength. Even a habit that's good to have in one set of circumstances can become unhelpful and self-defeating if it's too rigidly established to flex and yield when circumstances change and that habit becomes less appropriate to have.

Anyone born and raised in the United States likely has an interesting habit. When we prepare to cross a street we tend to look left first for traffic. Then we look right. This is only natural, since by the rules of the road in the United States, oncoming traffic on the near-side lane on a two-way street comes from the left. When I'm about to cross a street, look left and see nothing coming, I often step off the curb before looking right. Most of the time, that's no problem. But it could become one.

Another philosopher visited my office fresh back from his first trip to London. Can you see what's coming? He couldn't, because he looked the wrong way. He said, "Tom, I almost got killed my first day in England." I asked, "What happened? Was there a terrorist bombing?" He said, "No, I just left the hotel for the first time, looked left, stepped off the curb, and a bus almost took my head off." I replied, "Thanks for capturing for me the human condition." He said "What?" I explained, "A habit you had that was a perfectly healthy form of behavior in one set of circumstances became very dangerous when circumstances changed. That is an image of the human condition in times of change." What worked in the past may not work in the future. We need to examine our habits for consistency with our goals as circumstances change.

Habit, if not resisted, soon becomes necessity.
St. Augustine (354–430)

We should be extremely careful about allowing bad habits to creep into our lives, whatever their origin. At an annual meeting for soccer coaches, one of the leaders came up to me and asked, "Why are good habits so much easier to break than bad habits?" I had never been asked that question before, but it's something we've all noticed. There appears to be an interesting difference between good and bad habits: Breaking a bad habit can be like trying to pull a big tree out of the ground. The long and tangled roots can seem to resist almost any amount of force. Good habits, by contrast, often just collapse in the face of the slightest temptation.

The explanation for this is actually fairly simple. Good habits are usually the result of perceptive thought, rational decision, and repetition. We read about the health benefits of exercise, and conclude we need a daily walk. Reflecting on medical claims about dietary fat, we resolve to change how we eat. We calculate that, to meet projected sales goals, we should make a certain number of calls each day. We pursue our new program, and after a few days or weeks of altered behavior, we have some good new habits.

Bad habits, by contrast, are usually not the offspring of logical thought and deliberation but of feeling, or sensation, plus repetition. It tastes good, so we eat it. And it was so good, we eat it again. It feels good, so we do it. And then we do it again.

Temptations to depart from a good habit usually appeal to the immediacy of one of our senses and offer fairly direct pleasure right away. This happens even when the pleasure is nothing more than the minor relief of convenience, or the temporary joy of lethargy. The good habit we're tempted to break is typically based in reason. And the negative consequences of falling into temptation and breaking that habit often can seem remote, abstract, and even avoidable. Add to this the fact that, unfortunately, in this world reason is often no match for feeling, and you have a decent explanation for why it's so easy to blow a good habit.

Our bad habits, by contrast, resist change precisely because they are rooted in the strength of feeling, emotion, or pleasurable sensation. It's hard to overcome this immediate power with rational conclusions about fairly remote benefits to be derived—possibly—by a contrary and less immediately enjoyable behavior. That's why it's better to avoid a bad habit than to have to deal with it later. But even the worst habits can be overcome.

FEAR AND INCONSISTENCY

Excessive fear is always powerless.
Aeschylus

In business, inconsistency sometimes originates with fear. A salesperson may not make a call because of a fear of failure, or may avoid meeting with an unhappy client from a fear of rejection or unpleasantness. Of course, the self-defeating nature of such behavior is evident. Without sales calls, there are no sales. The longer an already unhappy client has to wait, the worse the unpleasantness will be. Obviously, fear-based inconsistency is especially insidious when each action that's out of step with the relevant goals worsens the situation and increases the emotional pressure toward further inconsistency. The fewer the calls you make because of fear, the more your success depends on the next call, which gives you even more to fear.

A financial executive once told me this story from his life. Fresh out of the army, he felt like Superman. But he became a salesman, and suddenly the telephone was Kryptonite. He was supposed to be making cold calls, but he hesitated out of a fear of rejection. Bullets he could handle. Failure was different. Every morning he would put off the phone calls he should have been making, and postpone them until the afternoon. Then, late in the day, he'd find new reasons to procrastinate. Days and weeks would pass like this. The phone seemed to weigh sixty pounds. He'd pick it up to make a call, and put it right back down. He was even aware that this was inconsistent with his own goals. But he was paralyzed by fear.

Courage is resistance to fear,
mastery of fear—not absence of fear.
Mark Twain (1835–1910)

One day this young man sat in a traffic jam on his way home from work and noticed a bumper sticker on the car in front of him. It said, simply, DARE TO BE GREAT. It was a long traffic jam, so he had time to reflect deeply on that message. When he got home, he decided to make his own version on a piece of posterboard. The next day he took it into work and taped it on the wall above the phone. The effect was immediate. He started making calls right away. Rejection was suddenly not a problem. Before he even registered hearing a no, he'd be dialing the next number, shooting for a yes. In very little time he turned his business life around and gave himself the consistency of action he needed to succeed and ascend to the top-management position for all the firm's offices in town.

THE POWER OF CONSISTENT PURSUIT

How can we best deal with the problem of inconsistent action? There is a great, effective strategy available. If we vividly imagine the worst possible consequences of that behavior, remind ourselves just as vividly of what we are pursuing and why, and warn ourselves about the dangers of self-deception, we will be able to defeat the scourge of inconsistency.

A good scare is worth more to a man than good advice.
E. W. Howe (1853–1937)

There's no more effective way to deal with bad habits than the experience of a disaster they've produced. We're most motivated to change our ways when we're forced to face consequences we don't want. But the good news is that we don't have to wait until our bad habits have disastrous results. We can use the power of the imagination to simulate, shock, and warn. A vivid vision of virtual disaster can be nearly as powerful as the real thing for reorienting behavior and getting us back on track.

An ounce of prevention is always good: If we keep our goals in view and remind ourselves of where we're going, we'll be better able to spot any temptation toward inconsistency for what it is. If we do fall into an inconsistent act, we should be honest with ourselves about what's happened, reflect on the danger of what we've done, and renew our resolve as strongly as possible to move again in the right direction. We may even need to enlist another person's help. We should do everything we can never to let a detrimental habit form.

In the end, we need to remember that the only power on earth capable of resisting inconsistency is the power of the will. We each have within us the willpower needed to change any personal behavior. Sometimes we can resist temptation and eliminate old habits through the sheer power of our own resolve. At other times we need external help, but even in those cases, we already have the willpower sufficient to seek and use that outside assistance.

A man can do all things if he but wills them.

Leon Battista Alberti (1404–1472)

Your power of will is great. It's much greater than you realize. But still, to make use of it you may have to draw on other inner powers, like the power of the imagination. I have come to believe the imagination is the single greatest natural power in human life, given to us precisely to empower us to meet difficult challenges. Draw on the power of imagination, draw on positive relationships, give yourself pep talks, and make use of whatever other support you have access to in order to leverage the power of your own will. In the end, it is your own willpower that will determine whether you march forward to attain your goals or allow short-term temptations and groundless fears to derail your progress. Every challenge is, ultimately, one way or another, a matter of the will. And only you can decide how you will meet the challenge with the strength you have.

The will of a man is his happiness.

J. C. F. von Schiller

THE POWER OF CONSISTENT PURSUIT

Why is consistency a fundamental condition of success? The answer to this is almost a no-brainer. If my goal is some simple, fairly immediate state—say, I want to drink from my coffee cup—then I just reach over, pick up the cup, and sip. I don't worry about considerations of consistency in my behavior. But notice that if I had acted inconsistently with my goal—if, despite wanting a drink and setting as a goal the target of sipping from my coffee cup, I had left the room instead of reaching over to the cup—I would not have attained my goal as immediately as I did.

An example like this can seem silly. It's just when we set more challenging and less immediate goals that issues of consistency typically come up. The more difficult and remote the goal is, the more important matters of consistency are.

He who would arrive at the appointed end
must follow a single road and not wander through many ways.
Seneca

Any journey of achievement involves goal pursuit through time. The higher the goals we set ourselves, the more work it will take to achieve them. Confident expectation has to come into play. Planning is necessary. Patience and persistence are required. A gardener has to water his plants faithfully. A writer needs to return to the desk, day after day. A salesperson has to cultivate new clients. Focus is crucial. And follow-through is everything. Success often comes from keeping at the same task, or the same series of tasks, and not letting up. The art of consistency is relevant to everything.

No great thing is created suddenly.
Epictetus

Temptations to take a short-cut or the easy way out will always be there, but they have to be resisted. The great Reformation theologian Martin Luther once said, in reference to temptations, that you can't keep the birds of the air from flying around your head, but you can keep them from building a nest in your hair.

There's no need to feel bad about undergoing temptations. Everyone is tempted, at some time or other, to stray from the path they've chosen. Don't even come down too hard on yourself for a single isolated slipup. It happens. In fact, to blame yourself for having worries, or for feeling tempted into inconsistent behavior, or even for experiencing a small slip of inconsistent action, would be like a pilot blaming his plane for turbulence, or a driver blaming his car for potholes. Life contains this stuff. We can't totally avoid it. But whatever happens—whether you run into a stretch of second-guessing, an onslaught of temptation, a paralysis of fear, or actually go down for a fall—simply pick yourself up again, strengthen your resolve, and face forward toward your goal. The process must go on. Progress must be made, little by little. Even our temptations and our stumblings can give us occasion to gain self-knowledge, renew our vision for where we need to go, and recommit ourselves to the process of getting there.

> *As the Sandwich Islander believes that the strength and valor of the enemy he kills passes into himself, so we gain the strength of the temptation we resist.*
>
> Ralph Waldo Emerson

The power of consistent pursuit, to the extent that we can attain it, is to wear down the obstacles in our way and to make the path to our goal as smooth as we are capable of making it.

CHAPTER

12 Sending the Right Signals

Consistency in moving toward achieving our goals in harmony with our values is not to be thought of as blindly repetitive behavior, the same today as yesterday, the same tomorrow as always. Whenever we speak of the virtue of consistency, it's important to make this as clear as possible. It's vital to have this straight in our own minds as well. Consistency is not the same thing as habit. Habits can produce behavior consistent with our goals, or inhibit the sort of consistency we need in order to move forward most effectively toward those goals.

VISION CONSISTENCY

If we pursue a relatively unchanging goal throughout changing circumstances, we often need to adapt our tactics as we go. If the goal is emended, if the target itself is moving, then it's even more obvious that our tactics will have to change. Consistency with our overall vision of where we want to go does not require that we be rigidly unchanging, despite our circumstances. In a changing world, it demands the opposite—it requires that we not get stuck in a rut, but rather become ever adaptive. Consistency and change can go hand in hand, and often do. This is what I mean by vision consistency.

Every master knows that the
material teaches the artist.
Ilya Ehrenburg (1891–1967)

This distinction between consistency and sameness is crucial to communicate to the people with whom we pursue important goals. By asking for consistency we are not asking that they be set in all their ways. We are sometimes asking that they set and reset their ways frequently, within the bounds of any ongoing strategies we have agreed on and consonant with all the basic values that we share, to get us closer to the goal. As we seek true consistency in everything we do, it's important to send the right signals out to everyone else involved.

We also need to send ourselves the right signals about what vision consistency is and is not. Vision consistency—goal-centered and value-governed consistency—is not by nature mainly backward-looking. Its essence is not in repeating past behaviors. It is forward-looking. Where do we want to be next week, next month, next year? And what will it take to get us there? We'll face enough obstacles anyway without placing new ones in our paths through actions inconsistent with our goals or values.

As we work toward the attainment of difficult targets, it sometimes becomes very hard to remain consistent with our overall vision. Consistency can be a challenging creative endeavor in rapidly changing times. But the effort at consistency itself builds momentum and becomes easier as we progress.

All things are difficult before they are easy.
Thomas Fuller (1608–1661)

THE CHALLENGE OF ADVENTURE

In any quest for success, we're faced with a balancing act. We have to combine an open adaptiveness of our behavior with an ongoing commitment to fundamental values and overall life goals in everything we do. In any pursuit of achievement, new behavior is required by novel conditions, new goals, and new problems. To be opportunistic in the best sense is to be creative and innovative—to be mentally, emotionally, and behaviorally adaptive as we face new situations. But this is not the same as becoming relativistic in our values—doing whatever seems to work in new circumstances, regardless of whether it comports with our most fundamental beliefs. Vision consistency means adapting and creating within a stable framework of basic values and beliefs. Things can go wrong when people fail to adapt, and they can go very wrong when people give up too much of who they are and what they believe just to fit in to a new environment in which they find themselves.

A windmill is eternally at work to accomplish one end, although it shifts with every variation of the weathercock, and assumes ten different positions in a day.

Charles Caleb Colton (1780–1832)

A senior manager in a large corporation wants to go out on his own and start a small company. He views it as a new adventure long overdue in his life. But he can fail quickly by bringing too many of his big-organization habits of thinking and acting into the new situation. This is failure through lack of flexibility, lack of adaptiveness. That sort of inflexibility ends up creating behavior inconsistent with the goals and strategies the new context demands.

On the other hand, a willingness to adapt should not lead to a fundamental malleability. Take the example of a young man who leaves his small community and moves to a big city to chase his dreams, and also leaves behind the small-town values that alone would keep those big-city dreams from turning sour. In this case, flexibility has gone too far and has been transformed into relativism. From this, some form of personal failure is a nearly guaranteed consequence.

The challenge is to remain deeply true to yourself while changing as required by any new pursuits that are in fact right for you. That's why attaining healthy consistency is an art. There are no simple formulas for spotting it in all situations, or for achieving it in all possible circumstances. That is the great balancing act of a wise and healthy life of proper achievement. Whatever our challenges and hopes might be, it's important that we remain who we most deeply are as we grow into what we are capable of becoming. If we maintain a firm grip on our most basic values, there will be certain ways in which we rightly refuse to change, regardless of the rewards that might be promised.

Remember you have only one soul, only one death, only one life. If you do this, there will be many things about which you care nothing.

St. Teresa of Avila (1515–1582)

WHAT CONSISTENCY COMMUNICATES

Consistent action sends a message: "I really believe in this and I'm committed to it." Inconsistent action also sends a message, or rather a set of messages: "I don't really believe in this," "I don't really want it, despite what I say," or "I don't think this is worth the effort after all." Other people who are being asked to join with us to work toward a goal are always watching to see whether we really mean it or not. Why should someone else sign on to our project if we really don't believe in it or intend to see it through?

A company president told me that he had launched out into a new adventure in his large organization in an effort to change long-term patterns in the corporate culture, and that as a part of this, he had instituted a new paradigm of teamwork for all of the business. He was preaching the need for team initiatives throughout the company, and altering all his incentive and reward systems accordingly. He confided to me one day that he sometimes worried he might have overlooked some program within the company still focused on individuals rather than teams. His fear was that if employees noted any inconsistency at all in the company's policies or procedures, they wouldn't say "Well, they just haven't gotten to retooling this particular system yet," or "Here's something they've overlooked so far and neglected to integrate into the new program," but instead, their reaction would be "Aha! They're not really serious about this new team vision stuff after all!"

Why are people seemingly on the lookout for any little inconsistency, and so ready with the "Aha!" response when they find one? It is in part because people tend to trust our words only when they're backed up with the right actions. And whenever people are being asked to make changes in the way they do things, changes that may initially be difficult, they are reluctant to join in wholeheartedly until they know that there's not a hidden agenda, or that management really means what it says. Little things communicate big messages. Others won't be confident that we mean what we say unless they see us acting consistently with that message.

I have always thought the actions of men
the best interpreters of their thoughts.
John Locke (1632–1704)

A few years ago I came to realize that I was traveling too much. I was flying all over the country giving talks to business and professional groups about the relevance of ancient wisdom to modern life. I'd be away for two or three nights, and back home for one or two, then off again. I was having a great time with every audience. But I was missing my family. A lot. And I could tell that when I was home, family life was not what it was capable of being. My wife and children were having to develop their own routines without me. When I returned, I would often feel like a visitor. I decided I needed to cut back on travel and spend more time with the family. I made that a goal, and a priority.

Notice a couple of things here. First, we often discover our proper limits in life by crossing them. We go too far, and looking back, see where we should have stopped. As a result, we find ourselves living in a way that is inconsistent with some of our deepest and dearest values. I was in such a position, and I let this generate a new goal. But the goal was vague. I wanted to spend more time with my family. What exactly did that mean? How should it cause me to act on a given day, and in response to a given invitation to travel? It wasn't at all clear.

Vague goals cannot reliably motivate specific behavior. Six months after making my new resolution to stay home more, I came to realize I was still traveling too much. There would always be a special reason to accept a particular invitation, a reason that made sense at the time. But the sum total of all the agreements to leave home to speak was that once again I was staring out the window of an airplane, wondering what had happened.

People make this mistake in their business lives all the time. I have been told in various settings that a company had the new goal of getting closer to its customers. But what exactly does this mean? A company that goes no further than to say something like that is indeed articulating a new ideal, but it's not specific enough to really count as a new goal. It's too vague. How would they know if they had attained it, or even gotten closer to it? As we saw in earlier chapters, we need a clear conception of what we want in every situation where we are able to set goals. Specificity is a key.

I had announced to my wife and children that I wanted to travel less and spend more time at home. I had told them I wanted to be with them more. But I was not acting like it. I was acting inconsistently with what I had said I would be doing. And that affected how they regarded me. My conduct made it look like going on one more trip, and giving one more speech, was always more important than being with them. And when I was home, I found myself in work and leisure routines that did not include my children enough. I was missing the intimacy I knew was there to be experienced. It was all because I did not set clear enough goals, and didn't make enough effort to act consistently with my new decisions about family life.

The best of intentions can be eroded by vagueness and habit. Vagueness in our goals prevents us from recognizing inconsistency when it occurs. And habit insidiously pushes old behavior into new circumstances, even when we have vowed that things would henceforth be different.

A just cause is not ruined by a few mistakes.

Fyodor Dostoyevsky

I can report all this failure on my part with some equanimity now because I finally have it under control. I have more specific goals, having set a numerical cap on trips per month and a limit on consecutive nights away from home. I also have more specific goals concerning time I spend with my wife and children when I am at home. And the results have been great. When my behavior was inconsistent with my words, it communicated unfortunate signals to my family. My current hard-won consistency makes my words more credible and my deepest commitments more obvious.

There is a new unity in my family life. My wife and children feel it just as I do. And I attribute this in various ways to my attaining greater consistency in my actions, and so greater consistency in what those actions communicate to the other members of the family. I have learned over and over, in many ways, that in any endeavor, even the smallest things matter.

God is in the details.

Ludwig Mies van der Rohe (1886–1969)

Let me return for a moment to a point I've made earlier, and in a quite general manner. As it has often been remarked that success is a journey and not a destination, the same is also true for each of the universal conditions of success that we're considering. And this is particularly crucial to understand in the case of consistency. In real life, for even the wisest of people, consistency is a challenging journey, and never a destination at which we fully arrive. Our circumstances are always changing, however slightly or profoundly, and with every new step we must learn to monitor our behavior afresh for its harmony with our deepest goals and values. As in music, the harmony that is vision consistency involves a dynamic, sympathetic resonance among disparate elements of our lives, as well as with external forces that impinge on us. Its precise form will often change over time, and can sometimes be difficult to attain anew, but its power in every goal pursuit, over the long run, is astonishing.

Harmony makes small things grow;
lack of harmony makes great things decay.
Sallust (86–35 B.C.)

The fourth condition of success says that we need to attain a stubborn consistency in little things as well as in big things as we pursue our goals. This greatly magnifies our efforts, powerfully enlists the aid of others in our enterprises, and helps everyone around us to know and understand us better. The art of consistency, as difficult as it sometimes might be, is one worth mastering.

PART 5

THE ART OF COMMITMENT

As to the artists,
do we not know that only he whom
love inspires has the light of fame?
He whom love touches not walks in darkness.

Plato

CHAPTER

13

Enthusiasm

CONDITION 5 OF THE 7 Cs:

*We need an emotional **Commitment** to the importance of what we're doing.*

Look up, laugh loud, talk big,
keep the colour in your cheek and the fire in your eye,
adorn your person, maintain your health,
your beauty and your animal spirits.
William Hazlitt (1778–1830)

Some of our adventures in life are journeys we choose. Others are thrust upon us. It's easier to be emotionally committed to the importance of what we're doing if we've freely chosen our course, reflectively deciding to launch into something new. It can be very hard to engage our hearts fully in a new enterprise when it has come our way unsought and unexpected.

You can suddenly find yourself in the job market, or facing the challenge of single parenthood, or relocating to a part of the country you know nothing about to work on a project you were just assigned. You confront a new adventure you never asked for and can easily feel bewildered, unsure, or even depressed. But an emotional commitment to the challenge you confront is just as crucial for success in any endeavor, whether it's something you've selected for yourself or not. An active engagement of the heart is one of the universal facilitators of satisfying success in any difficult enterprise.

Enthusiasm and excellence are often found paired in human history, and they're an unbeatable combination in the world now. Preparation and passion together yield power. The greatest accomplishments in any field of human endeavor tend to be achieved by people who work hard, work smart, and work with energetic enthusiasm, believing in what they're doing from deep in their hearts. Any adventure in life is enhanced immensely by inner enthusiasm, an emotional commitment that energizes the day and refreshes us for whatever new challenges we face. There is an art to passionate commitment. And it is an art that can be learned.

Let me give you a memorable example of real enthusiasm in action. In his famous book *The Double Helix,* James Watson describes a scientific meeting in which the great Nobel–Prize winning chemist Linus Pauling was to present his new model of the structure of proteins to a number of students and professional colleagues:

> Pauling's talk was done with his usual flair. The words came out as if he had been in show business all his life. A curtain kept his model hidden until near the end of his lecture, when he proudly unveiled his latest creation. Then, with his eyes twinkling, Linus explained the specific characteristics that made his model uniquely beautiful.
>
> This show, like all of his dazzling performances, delighted the younger students in attendance. There was no one like Linus in all the world. The combination of his prodigious mind and his infectious grin was unbeatable.
>
> Several fellow professors, however, watched this performance with mixed feelings. Seeing Linus jumping up and down on the demonstration table and moving his arms like a magician about to pull a rabbit out of his shoe made them feel inadequate. If only he had shown a little humility, it would have been so much easier to take!

This is enthusiasm. This is energy. This is emotional commitment.

He is the true enchanter whose spell operates,
not upon the senses, but upon the imagination and the heart.
Washington Irving (1783–1859)

I shouldn't use this example from the life of Linus Pauling without clarifying two things right away. First, you don't have to dance on tables to be an enthusiast. You don't need to be a rambunctious, over-the-top, performing extrovert. You do have to be passionate, believe from the heart in what you're doing, and let that passion show through. Enthusiasm by its very nature seeks to communicate itself. The enthusiast wants others to share his passion, and his commitment.

A second, and very important, point. This kind of passion, the passion of enthusiastic emotional commitment, is thoroughly compatible with a proper degree of personal humility. Enthusiasm is not the same thing as arrogance, haughtiness, or presumptuousness, although it typically contains at least a small measure of good old-fashioned chutzpah. The enthusiast need not have a closed mind, but can be very open to learning new perspectives and changing his strategies as he pursues his vision.

THE HUMBLE ENTHUSIAST

An arrogant, haughty person demands attention for himself. An enthusiastic person would rather draw your attention to the object of his excitement—the innovative model of protein structure, a new product line, a novel service concept, an extraordinary idea.

Humility, like darkness, reveals the heavenly lights.
Henry David Thoreau (1817–1862)

An enthusiast is emotionally possessed, passionately moved by the importance of what he has discovered, or what he can contribute. To be an enthusiast in the best possible way, a person has to be a bit transparent, or at least translucent, so that the glow of The Idea, The Possibility, The Job, or The Relationship that excites him can shine through. An arrogant person is opaque. Look at him and what you see is: him. Arrogance is ultimately self-referential. It can be energetic, but its energy is self-manufactured and self-directed. It doesn't flow into others naturally, but assaults them with bursts of insistence.

We don't usually feel the deep attractive energy of the universe flowing freely through the life of an utterly arrogant individual. But this is exactly what we feel in the presence of a genuine enthusiast. Authentic, natural enthusiasm allows a light to shine through the person caught up in its energy. It conveys to others some of the magic that has generated it.

Enthusiasm is that secret and harmonious spirit which hovers over the production of genius, throwing the reader of a book, or the spectator of a statue, into the very real ideal presence whence these works have really originated.
Isaac D'Israeli (1766–1848)

The arrogant person says, "Look at me." The enthusiastic person says, "Look at this." Ironically, we're attracted to enthusiasm and repelled by conceit. And as we are drawn to the enthusiast we are drawn to his ideas. If they are indeed good ideas, then in finding ourselves attracted to them, we are in turn further attracted to that person whose enthusiasm called our attention to these new ideas in the first place.

Enthusiasm and arrogance are not a natural mix at all, unless, of course, you are yourself the main focus of your enthusiasm. A healthy enthusiasm is always outward-looking. And being a humble enthusiast certainly doesn't require you to downplay the importance or excitement of what you're doing. The humble person just feels very lucky or blessed to be doing it.

Humble enthusiasm combined with a healthy self-confidence is an attitudinal combination that ought to be required equipment for anyone setting out on a new and challenging endeavor. The humble person is open to learning new things. The self-confident person is open to doing new things. The enthusiast has the wind at her back, and that extra spring in her step that will help her persist long enough to learn and do everything that the new challenge makes possible.

The higher we are placed, the more humbly should we walk.

Cicero

Rudy Pensa was a young guitarist in Argentina, dreaming of America. He had seen pictures of many of the world's most famous musicians buying guitars in the fabled music stores of Forty-eighth Street in New York City, and he wanted with all his heart to work there. In 1974, he arrived in the land of his dreams with one suitcase and a hundred dollars. He found his way straight to Forty-eighth Street, entered a music store, introduced himself, explained his musical background, and asked for work. He was given a shovel and told to clean out the basement. The work was hard, exhausting, and dirty, and not at all what he had expected, but he was on the street he loved, and no job was beneath him. He did his work well, with all the energy that his enthusiasm for life, guitars, and Forty-eighth Street could spark, and his efforts paid off.

I heard his story recently, from the man himself, while standing in my favorite store on Forty-eighth Street, Rudy's Guitar Stop. Along one wall are the most beautiful vintage instruments I've ever seen. I wondered aloud how he finds all these amazing and rare works of art. He explained, with the happiest passion in his Argentinean voice that I've ever heard, "I love guitars, Tom. And when you love guitars, guitars will find you."

He then regaled me and my son with stories of rare, priceless guitars that found him and fell into his arms over the years. His eyes lit up and he nearly danced as he described instruments so beautiful that "they would make you cry."

Rudy loves guitars. And he loves what he does. Catching sight of me admiring a particularly striking old arched-top guitar, Rudy quickly took it out of its glass exhibition case and turned it over so that I could see the wood grain on its back. "Look at that, just look at that," he said, "God made that!"

Rudy's enthusiasm is contagious. And his personal humility is inspirational. He has never called my attention to the beautiful new instruments in the store that bear the name Pensa Guitars. And yet he seems to live in constant celebration of all the good things success has brought into his life. I can just hear his lilting accent as he exclaims, "This is not work, it's love!"

A great artist can paint a great picture on a small canvas.
C. D. Warner (1829–1900)

Every time I go to New York City, I try to visit Rudy's Guitar Stop, not only to see and play the amazing guitars, but just as much to soak in a dose of Rudy's enthusiastic love for what he is doing. If you love guitars, I am now convinced, guitars will find you. And this power of attraction works universally. But, most important, if you love what you do, the right people will find you. And they will want to be part of your adventure too.

PRIDE AND HUMILITY

Think for a moment about the most successful, adventurous people you know or have read about. They tend to be tremendous enthusiasts, people of great emotional commitment. No one explores a remote jungle or climbs a challenging mountain with an attitude of detached indifference. White-water rafting, spelunking, and cross-country cycling are not for the apathetic.

In addition to being emotionally committed to what they're doing, most adventurous people are also proud of what they're up to, as well as of what they've already accomplished. But that pride, at its best, is very different from any type of in-your-face arrogance.

These distinctions are so important that we should explore just a bit more some of the most salient aspects of humility and pride as they relate to enthusiasm and other forms of emotional commitment. Many people seem to think of humility and pride as opposite ends of a spectrum of possible states of self-esteem:

This can be very misleading. Proper pride in who you are, in what you're doing, and in how you're doing it is surely a good thing. Portraying pride and humility as opposites is apt to make you think of humility as a bad thing. Humility begins to look a little bit like low self-esteem.

If, on the other hand, you appreciate humility as a virtue, a good and admirable attitude to have, then this oppositional picture makes any sort of pride look like a bad thing—as if pride were the same thing as arrogance, which it is not.

Maybe a different portrayal is more revealing:

At one end of this spectrum is low self-esteem, a lack of pride in one's work, self-diminishment, and a feeling of being immersed in triviality. The other extreme is an overweening, haughty, inappropriate, self-aggrandizing, self-fixated pridefulness. The Aristotelian-style virtue would be at the spectrum's midpoint, balancing a proper pride and dignity—a deep and confident sense of importance—with a true humility and thankfulness for what one has that also allows a full respect for the importance of other people and their different tasks and talents. Humility is a virtue the ancient Greek philosophers seem not to have fully recognized as such. It is the Judeo-Christian tradition, and in particular, a central strand of Christian theology, that historically brought humility to our attention. Humility, it turns out, is one of the greatest of the virtues. If you have it, you can indeed be proud of it.

Humility is just as much the opposite of self-abasement as it is of self-exaltation.
Daq Hammarskjöld (1905–1961)

How does enthusiasm relate to humility? As we noted earlier, a proper enthusiasm, like humility, puts you in the *background,* so your ideas can come to the *fore.* Also like humility, its proper companion attitude, enthusiasm can be seen as the midpoint on another spectrum, one showing levels of a person's ability to be engaged, interested, and involved in something he's doing:

When I mention enthusiasm as an important factor in success, I am not endorsing an unbalanced, crazy, out-of-your-mind, out-of-control, unhealthy nuclear-meltdown fixation of emotional energy on your goal, although if I had to err on one end of the spectrum, I have to admit that I'd find even this preferable to a glum, plodding, zombie-like boredom. But you can go all out, you can even go to some extremes, without necessarily falling off the edge. The enthusiastic person need not and should not be a crazed lunatic bereft of any sense of proportion.

But even an extremely energetic enthusiasm can be thought of as an Aristotelian-style virtue, a midpoint, a broad plateau rising high between two valleys, something we could a bit playfully characterize as a sort of extreme mean between meaner extremes. The enthusiastic person who is also well balanced, psychologically healthy, and thoroughly in touch with rationality embodies a virtue that brings with it tremendous possibility and amazing power.

The world belongs to the enthusiast who keeps cool.
William McFee (1881–1966)

If my little diagrams here are roughly accurate, I think they indicate that you can be an enthusiast and still embody an appropriate measure of personal humility. It's indeed an art to attain this balance, but it certainly can be done. You can be excited about the importance of what you're doing without that excitement leading you into inappropriate arrogance. And you can be enthusiastic about whatever you're doing without being obnoxiously monomaniacal.

I've thought long and hard to come up with these conclusions, and I guess it would be very natural at this point to want to tell you that I'm very proud of what I've learned about humility. I'm also humbled by it. And the final result of all this is that I'm more enthusiastic about my own enthusiasm than ever before!

CHAPTER

Boredom, Exuberance, and Dignity 14

Boredom is, ironically, interesting. Why are so many people so easily bored? We live at the most exciting time in human history. There are more opportunities for creativity, growth, and personal development than ever before, and they're all around us. Things are changing at an extraordinary pace. The world is shrinking into one global economy. Technology is altering our lives every few months in some new, unexpected way. Yet too many people seem to sleepwalk through their work, drift through their relationships, and generally live one long psychological yawn.

Is not life a hundred times too short
for us to bore ourselves?
Friedrich Nietzsche

In this chapter I want to analyze a common reason for boredom, a lack of interest and a lack of enthusiasm, on the job and in life. I also want to offer a philosophical remedy that can help any of us to master the art of commitment.

A PHILOSOPHICAL ANALYSIS OF BOREDOM

The existentialist philosopher Jean-Paul Sartre once analyzed boredom as involving "simultaneously too much and too little." A bit of meditation on this apparent paradox may be revealing.

Have you ever seen a child surrounded by hundreds of toys, books, and electronic games plaintively cry out, "I'm bored"? Too much and too little. But wait a minute. The "too much" is clear. What's the "too little"?

Perhaps the flip side of the coin, the hidden reality behind that pile of stuff. It may be that kids get bored when they are given too much ready-made comfort, too much convenience, too much easy entertainment. What they have too little of is meaningful, creative challenge. I remember hearing my parents say many times that when they were young, when children had to work hard around the house or on the farm and had to make their own toys from whatever could be found, nobody had time to get bored. When they weren't working or playing, they were too tired to be bored.

Human beings in primal societies, living at the edge of survival, seem not to know boredom. They're too busy hunting, farming, gathering, and celebrating the fruits of their efforts to be bored. Cave art appears to indicate a prehistoric fascination with life in the natural world. Primal humans and nonhuman animals seem to share a fullness of existence that avoids the simultaneously too much and too little that Sartre identified as the universal ingredients of boredom.

Man is the only animal that can be bored.
Erich Fromm (1900–1980)

There is indeed a formula for boredom. Too much time on our hands with too little to do that really engages our creative energies. Or too much to do that has too little meaning or importance to us. Or, too much work that we have too little personal creative control over. Too much of a good thing with too little variety. Too much success that comes too easily, with too few challenges. Always, somehow, too much and too little at the same time. This seems to be the universal recipe for that unhappy state of mind.

Boredom itself is one of the most potent recipes for death—a death of the spirit and even a death of the body. It can be the death of a relationship. And it can kill a business. It is, at its essence, an attitude of lifelessness. And that's exactly where it leads. A bored person is not a person emotionally committed to the importance of what he or she is doing. A person burdened with this malady is not in the right mindset for producing future success at anything.

Work spares us from three great evils:
boredom, vice, and need.
Voltaire (1694–1778)

We need to ask what it takes to move anyone from just going through the motions to enthusiastic emotional commitment. This may seem like a difficult question, but I've come to believe that it has a very simple answer. It takes two things: *Interest* plus *desire* equals *emotional commitment.*

ARE YOU INTERESTED?

Let's begin with the basic mental state of interest. A person can't be emotionally committed to the importance of what she's doing without a high level of interest in her work.

We need to ask how an individual who is not fascinated by her job can become more interested in it, or how anyone can gain a higher level of interest in an ongoing relationship. How can you recapture your first love for what you do, where you are, or the person you're with? It just takes a shift of perspective. And sometimes all this requires is a shift of attention.

No situation is intrinsically interesting or intrinsically boring. Of course, some situations are better than others, but boredom and fascination ultimately have to do not so much with our outer circumstances as with our inner attitudes. Proof of this is available all around us.

I've seen two people in exactly the same situation, at the same time, but one of them was fascinated and the other was bored to death. Okay, I'll come clean. They were students in one of my classes, on a day of fairly technical philosophical argument. Same externals, different internals. Same circumstances, but different attitudes. Boredom and interest levels ultimately are determined by the mind.

The mind is its own place, and in itself
Can make a heav'n of hell, a hell of heav'n.
John Milton (1608–1674)

You can help another person, or even yourself, make that switch of perspective. Does the work you're doing match your talents and tastes? Is it challenging? Does it push you to the limits of your present development and on to further growth and learning? If not, can you do something about that?

Can you find anything new about your work to enjoy? Can you

work at it in a new way, developing some new skill or knowledge? Can you, in your own mind, put it into a bigger picture where you are able to see its importance in a new way? Can you reconceive it as an important part of your adventure through life? Can you connect it up with things that you already care about and love?

Maybe you won't be able to conquer a particular problem with boredom at work, or in a relationship, until you renew your general zest for life. Have you thought enough about the wonder of life in general, and about the wonder that is your life in particular? Or about the fact that you're here on this earth for so short a time? And what about the opportunities that each new day can bring you to touch and affect other people's lives for the better? Maybe you need to ask yourself whether you're emotionally embracing life as it deserves to be embraced.

The best philosophers have realized that wisdom is all about contextualization. How we contextualize our daily activities is up to us. Ultimately, each of us is responsible for putting our jobs, our relationships, and our lives into the right philosophical perspective, in such a way as to connect up with the things that, deep down, we love most and that matter to us the most.

The love of life is necessary to the
vigorous prosecution of any undertaking.
Samuel Johnson

I need to ask myself regularly: Am I enjoying what I'm doing? Do I feel fulfilled by it? If not, either I need to change what I'm doing, or else I need to renew my deepest perspectives on exactly why I'm doing it.

We all need to find something interesting to do, either within the current framework of our jobs, or by expanding that framework. And if we can't do either of those things, we may need to find a completely new outlet for our energies. But we ought to be very careful about making radical external changes before we have tried the techniques of internal renewal. It is a good rule in life to work on the inner before the outer whenever possible. Only then will any outer changes make the difference we want them to make.

Let's reflect a bit more on why something—anything—is interesting. Typically, we don't think something is really interesting unless we think it's important. This touches a nerve for a lot of people. When I go around the country speaking about enthusiasm and emotional commitment, I often hear people say: "But how can I get worked up about what I'm doing when most of the day is pretty routine? I'm supposed to be excited about the same old phone calls and paperwork? Look, fireworks don't go off around here very often. We just do what we have to do to make it through the day."

The measure of an enthusiasm
must be taken between interesting events.
It is between bites that the lukewarm angler loses heart.
Edwin Way Teale (1899–1980)

Let's be realistic. Not every day brings obviously dramatic, scintillating, glamorous developments into our lives. But so what? Who's to say what is and is not important? So your life is filled with little things? Does "little" equal "trivial and unimportant"? I don't think so. Does "little" mean "boring"? The greatest thinkers and their wise companions have told us something very different.

It has long been an axiom of mine
that the little things are infinitely the most important.
Sir Arthur Conan Doyle (1859–1930)

Size and importance are not the same thing. Appearance and significance can be very different. How big a job looks is not a reliable indication of how important it really is.

How important do your coworkers think your job is? How valuable and interesting does our society think your contribution to the world is? Guess what? It doesn't really matter. All that matters to your capacity to feel enthusiasm and commitment is how important you think it is. And that's entirely within your power. A task can be just as big or as important as you make it.

So much is a man worth as he esteems himself.
Rabelais (ca. 1494–1553)

Each of us has the power to endow our daily routines with significance, deep importance, and interest. If we develop a broader and deeper sense of respect for what we do, we put ourselves in an increasingly better position to become emotionally committed to it, day to day. No one else can determine for us the ultimate importance of our jobs, our relationships, or our lives. Valuation, respect, esteem, and deep emotional commitment must begin within us.

When we decide to value what we do, when we put our daily efforts into a bigger picture and envision the ongoing potential importance of even the smallest things, something surprising begins to happen. Other people start to share our perspective on the importance of our work. They begin to see what we do as having the importance we are giving it. This is one sometimes surprising result of practicing the art of commitment.

Respect yourself if you would have others respect you.
Balthasar Gracián

It takes a perceptive and philosophical soul to see the true deep importance of things, despite surface appearances. And it often takes a bold and imaginative soul to endow things with the ultimate significance they're capable of bearing. We're so full of prejudice about what's important and what's interesting. We're bowled over by the spectacular and the glamorous. We're unimpressed with the mundane and the little day-to-day advances our efforts most often bring. We hanker after instant-world-historical-significance. Every kid with a basketball wants to be the NBA MVP. Every guitar player craves the big stage, the recording contract, and MTV. With all those magazines needing all those cover photos every month, we sometimes secretly suspect, they're bound to get to me eventually.

Rightly viewed, no mean object is insignificant;
all objects are as windows, through which the
philosophic eye looks into infinitude itself.
Thomas Carlyle

The glare of the extraordinary blinds us to the potentially infinite importance of the ordinary. And the danger is great. We lose heart for our work before we can build any momentum with it. But heart is exactly what it takes to push any work along. Hardly anything worth doing is easy. Satisfying success never comes overnight. It's only when we make an emotional commitment to our work over the long haul that we position ourselves for success at anything challenging.

We must learn to take as much interest in the beginning and middle stages of an enterprise as in the later and more naturally exciting preliminaries of full-blown success. Many people fail for precisely this reason. They cannot maintain an interest in any process that doesn't immediately yield recognition, wealth, or measurable attainment. They get excited only about things that are obviously exciting. But the trick is to bring excitement to where that attitude needs to be created. Excited people are precisely the people who can create the most exciting results. Interested people are the people who create the most interesting results. They are able to begin from the beginning, find fascination in the process, and give passion to their work at every stage.

Do not despise the bottom rungs in the ascent to greatness.
Publilius Syrus

YOUR DEEPEST DESIRES

We're asking about emotional commitment and what it takes for us to be more enthusiastic about our work. We've seen first that in order to have genuine enthusiasm for what we're doing, we must find it interesting. And that won't happen unless we see it as important. But interest isn't enough. Not even fascination alone guarantees the kind of active emotional commitment that is a fundamental condition of success.

I like work: It fascinates me. I can sit and look at it for hours.
Jerome K. Jerome (1859–1927)

In order to have a deep and motivating emotional commitment to the importance of what we're doing, we must connect it up with something we strongly desire. Anyone can reenergize his work by reenvisioning a goal he deeply desires and imagining how his work can lead to that goal. The more vividly he envisions the goal, and the more strongly he desires its attainment, the more powerfully he will generate the emotional motivation he needs.

Where there is no desire, there will be no industry.
John Locke

Where there is no desire, motivation is flat. The heart is not engaged. Passion is not aroused. Why do so many people find themselves in this trough? The answer is simple. They have not been engaged in an ongoing process of imaginatively vivid goal setting and resetting. In our quest for excellence, in any lifelong adventure of success, regular renewal is of vital importance.

In a new job, it's not uncommon to be given new goals left and right. We're excited and enthusiastic. We're learning and being challenged to develop our skills and form new relationships. We see new possibilities all around and want to make them realities.

Then suppose we have some success, which is only natural on the wave of such energy. We're getting things done and getting comfortable with our new circumstances. We're feeling the rhythms. Our initial desires are satisfied. At least some of the things we had hoped for have come about. Now we have a problem.

We may just enjoy our success, celebrate our accomplishment, and begin to coast. Or we may take our success for granted and reach a plateau of performance, as we keep our heads down and become immersed in new routines. It could be that we see others having even greater success, and at some level we give up and brood. But whether we are relaxing, resenting the achievements of others, or just getting into partially passive routines, one of the greatest detriments to future success is a failure to continue setting new goals, renewing our vision of what we want, and rekindling the desire that alone propels us forward. Without new, rekindled desire, we won't likely have the motivation to launch out into the new adventures that are best able to lead us to ever more satisfying forms of success.

Desire attained is not desire
But as the cinders of the fire.
Sir Walter Raleigh (1554–1618)

I realize that not everyone agrees on the positive value that desire can have in human life. Philosophers have long noted that desire out of control is responsible for much of the misery in the world and a great deal of the unhappiness in people's lives. Buddhism consequently teaches that suffering arises from desire. If we had no desires, then nothing could disappoint us, and nothing could frustrate us. We are disappointed or frustrated only when the world is not as we desire it to be. So, there are voices within Buddhism then that call upon us to cease desiring. Eliminating desire is presented as the way to end suffering. Other ancient thinkers, the Greek Skeptics, went so far as to counsel a total cessation of belief. It's only when we believe our desires aren't met that we suffer mentally. Therefore, they advised, cease to believe and you can cease to suffer.

Naked I see the camp of those who desire nothing.
Horace

These recommendations are clearly extreme measures. Must we cease to have desires or beliefs in order to avoid the primary obstacles to happiness? I believe the answer is no. In order to avoid unnecessary suffering, all we need to do is shun false belief and inappropriate desire. All things considered, it's not at all clear that we would be better off if we avoided all suffering, even if that were possible. Suffering, when necessary and unavoidable, can build character, deepen us spiritually, and enhance our appreciation for elements of life we might otherwise overlook or neglect. All that we should seek to avoid is unnecessary suffering. But that is blocked by being careful with our beliefs, our desires, and our actions.

You must learn to desire what you would have.
Maxwell Anderson (1888–1959)

Our beliefs should always be responsible to the best evidence we can gather. Our desires should be governed by a healthy sense of self and a good set of values. And our actions should be consistent with our best beliefs and most fundamental commitments. Then we are doing all that is within our power to avoid unnecessary suffering.

But ask yourself a question: Is the avoidance of unnecessary suffering the only goal suitable for human beings? Is it a properly overriding goal, trumping every other aim we might have? I certainly don't think so. And I believe that the most philosophically insightful contemporary Buddhists also see that we are here not just to avoid the bad, but to accomplish the good. We are here not just for cessation, but rather for positive creation. And creation never comes about without both belief and desire. As long as our beliefs are true and our desires are good, the stronger they are, the more powerful they can be for good results in the world.

The Eastern wisdom that rings true is that our desires should never be allowed to become addictive cravings. And they should be directed toward goods that transcend the narrow concerns of the self, or bear a positive relationship to such goods. This deeper perspective is fully compatible with proper emotional commitments.

Heaven favors good desires.
Miguel de Cervantes (1547–1616)

We must learn to control our desires. And the stronger your desires are, the stronger you must also be to maintain control over them. Overly strong desire in any area of life, improperly controlled, can ruin a life. But strong desire appropriately directed can have extraordinarily positive results.

There is no inherent upper limit for the strength of desire, if desire is to play the positive role it is capable of playing in our lives. But the stronger it is, the stronger we must correspondingly be, or it will get control over us in an inappropriate and destructive way. If we cultivate moral transcendence, the ability to stand firm with a stable sense of self and right that rises above any contingency in the world, then we are free to cultivate the strongest possible desires to fuel our projects and prospects.

The person who cannot in any sense transcend, or rise above, his desires, while at the same time being motivated by them, is a person held captive by his wants, and is thereby captive to anything that can have power over the satisfaction of those wants. The person who can strongly desire a certain result and pursue it with all the passion that desire can generate, while at the same time transcending and thus relinquishing the emotional need to be responsible for and experience the benefits of what is desired, can move toward his goals with the maximum amount of personal power. Desires make us creative. Transcendence keeps us free.

Let us live while we live.
Philip Doddridge (1702–1751)

If we generate within ourselves a new interest in our work, and we cultivate desire in a positive way, we rekindle in ourselves the emotional commitment that's natural for achieving human beings to have, the heartfelt passion that's a fundamental condition for success in meeting life's challenges, and in that way we revive in ourselves the basis for really living and not just existing through the day. We can practice the art of commitment anytime. Why should we ever settle for anything less?

CHAPTER

The Power of Positive Feeling

15

Positive thinking has been praised for decades, and rightly so, because it leads to positive feeling. We can't be our best at work or at home unless we have very positive feelings about what we're doing there. Positive thinking and feeling are the basis for that most attractive of emotions and attitudes, enthusiasm. A positive attitude is the inner power that draws people out to new endeavors and on to new heights.

In every talk I give, I begin by asking the audience to name for me some of the great philosophers in history. Immediately, people start yelling out the names of Socrates, Plato, Aristotle, and Confucius. More often than not, someone eventually will shout "Yogi Berra!" So I suppose it's all right for me, as a philosopher, to quote that old catcher of insights, when he once said about baseball something true of life: "Ninety percent of the game is half mental."

He coulda been a Stoic. And actually, if Seneca or Epictetus had spent thousands of hours squatting in the hot summer sun, they might have put it the same way. Cicero himself once did say that, in this life, attitude is almost everything. The big question for many of us, then, is how to keep a positive attitude in everything we do.

THE PROBLEM OF NEGATIVITY

We often face a problem at work rarely discussed in management books. We're blocked from the positive attitude we need by negative emotional energy. In any job, things happen that produce bad feelings. We see the wrong person promoted. We lose a client. We hear "no" one time too many. We're going through a creative dry spell while pretending that everything's just fine. The market is challenging. We're doing more with less, and the pressures of downsizing are always in the back of our minds. Or, growth is coming too fast. The company's culture is changing in unpredictable ways. It's a sink-or-swim world and we're suddenly feeling a cramp.

The sources of negative emotions and a resulting negative attitude in all our relationships are almost too numerous to list. Neglect, hostility, an insensitive word, or a small act of apparent betrayal can cause negative reactions on a deep emotional level. We need to be careful how we respond to such things, or we fall into self-defeating patterns of emotional behavior.

We all have typical patterns of reacting to what happens around us. It's important to become more consciously aware of those patterns, and decide whether they are healthy. We always have the freedom to choose whether to indulge what seems to come naturally or, rather, to cultivate a different response.

Emotional reactions become habitual over time. By allowing ourselves to continue reacting to unwanted situations with negative feelings, we promote a tendency of inner behavior that can harden into a persistent attitude. And this inner behavior, with its accompanying attitude, eventually gives rise to more problems.

Check your passions that you may not be punished by them.

Epictetus

Our negative reactions of anger, resentment, and irritation often have a side to them that feels a little bit good. We're hurling an inner dart at the person or situation offending us. We think they deserve to be the object of anger. If no one were irritated at their behavior, they'd be getting away with something. We'll take care of this situation. So we fume. We tense up. We direct a mental tonality of disapproval in their direction—as if our inner emotions could inflict damage on anyone other than ourselves.

If you're all balled up in negative emotions, you're not going to be able to experience the positive attitudes and feelings that are most conducive to success and satisfaction in our world. Because of this, one of the most powerful acts, as well as one of the most powerful of all emotional states, is that of forgiveness.

To forgive much makes the powerful more powerful.

Publilius Syrus

A top manager in a very large organization once told me that they were having tremendous problems because of the simple fact that two of their vice presidents could not forgive each other for something that happened many years ago. No management tactics, motivational techniques, or strategic planning innovations had been able to overcome the ongoing damage that a lack of forgiveness between two people was inflicting on this big company.

THE POWER OF TRANSCENDENCE

Are negative emotions getting you down? Are they hindering someone who reports to you? Are they holding back your whole organization? Remember this: We have the power to rise above any negative situation. Tell yourself to transcend whatever is eating away at you. Put it into perspective, and realize how little it will mean in the long run. Wisdom is always about putting things into perspective. Take a deep breath, use positive imagination, and resist the self-defeating lure of the negative. As Yogi might say, "You won't get over it 'til you just get over it." Inner transcendence is the path to personal freedom.

The great Stoic philosopher and emperor of Rome, Marcus Aurelius, long ago pointed out, "Your life is what your thoughts make it." We can take charge of a situation most powerfully through first controlling our inner thoughts, emotions, and attitudes by deciding that we will not allow ourselves to be defeated in our own feelings. When we engage in positive emotional behavior, we clear full access for our deepest potential to have free play in the world.

Small-souled people make a big deal about small problems. Great-souled folks minimize those troubles in their hearts so they can best overcome them with their heads and hands. And then they take action. Positive action in turn cultivates positive attitude and positive emotion. As the philosopher William James discovered, the way we act and the way we talk can determine how we feel. But it all starts with the way we think.

In the ant's house, the dew is a flood.

Persian Proverb

Yogi was right. Ninety percent of the game is indeed half mental. Transcending negativity is vital, but we won't enjoy a strong positive attitude day to day unless we also renew our inner mental vision for what we're doing, give ourselves regular reminders of the nobility of our cause, and use our imaginations to enjoy at least a measure of the good we're doing in the world. Positive attitude ultimately depends on positive imagination. And that's entirely up to us.

TWO CONTRASTING STRATEGIES

Some people deal with frustration and disappointment by disengaging their emotions. To avoid the negative feelings their circumstances might cause, they try to avoid any feelings at all. They self-anaesthetize and sleepwalk through the day.

But there is no such thing as emotional neutrality. A lack of feelings itself can end up feeling pretty bad. The absence of negative emotion purchased by an absence of all emotion is an extremely negative psychological state to experience. And it's just as diminishing in the life of any individual who deserves a healthy measure of success. Lack of emotion is directly correlated to lack of success. And we all deserve better.

We often characterize a lack of any emotion at all as a state of "apathy," and that term derives from ancient roots that meant "without passion." A person without passion is without much hope, until it can be reignited in his heart.

Apathy can be overcome by enthusiasm,
and enthusiasm can be aroused by two things:
first, an idea which takes the imagination by storm;
and second, a definite, intelligible plan
for carrying that idea into action.
Arnold Toynbee (1889–1975)

The best cure for negative emotion is to displace it with positive emotion. But of course this is easier said than done. We can't just conjure positive feelings out of thin air. Positive emotion usually follows positive thinking, and positive thinking, to have fertile soil in which to grow, requires substantive, exciting ideas to support it and lead it forward. If we can rekindle our imaginations about the importance of what we're doing and can renew our vision for what's possible, we can begin a process of positive thinking and positive feeling, a process that will continue as long as we properly put our ideas into action with a practical plan of implementation. Small achievements will then renew us and prime us for bigger successes by reengaging our emotions. A productive course of setting and resetting goals, proceeding with confidence, concentrating on what it will take to meet those goals, and maintaining consistency in all our efforts will renew and nurture positive emotions and attitudes toward anything we're doing.

Nick Campbell is an engineer with Johnson & Johnson who has lived through this transformation. There was a time when he was all tied up in negative emotions at his job. He was working entirely for himself, thinking only about what was good for his career. But he wasn't getting the rewards or promotions he so desperately wanted. Every day was full of frustration. He hated Monday mornings days in advance. Coworkers even called him "B.A." for "bad attitude."

When he was twenty-nine, back surgery took him out of the fray and gave him time to stop and think about his life, his attitudes, and his mental approach to work. He came to realize that what he had been doing had not been working, and so he would have to change. Reading some of the best business and motivational literature, he began to understand the role of attitude and inner vision for outer success. As a result, he decided to use his imagination to envision his work in a whole new way, and that inner change made more of a difference than he ever could have imagined.

Do your work with your whole heart
and you will succeed—there is so little competition!
Elbert Hubbard

Nick began to think of himself as working for Campbell, Inc.—a wholly owned subsidiary of Johnson & Johnson. He took emotional ownership of the equipment in the lab, checking it at the end of the day to make sure it was clean and ready for the next morning. He then decided to see himself as being in the customer service business, and to view all of his associates as his customers. If he could help them solve their problems, he would have a successful day.

He started coming to work with a completely different attitude of expectant challenge, helpfulness, and emotional investment. And he started enjoying his work for the first time ever. People soon were thanking him for what he was doing. He was feeling a new pride in each day's work. And in the midst of this, he was summoned to his supervisor's office. At first he worried that perhaps he was being perceived as taking too much time from his primary assignments in his efforts to help solve others' problems. But there was no cause for anxiety. Because of what he was accomplishing for the whole department, and in recognition of his new level of commitment, Nick was promoted two levels. The prize that had eluded him when he sought it directly now was being handed to him for what he was accomplishing in service to the other people around him. And it was all a result of a new attitude that arose from new modes of thinking and gave birth to new emotions.

Beware of negative thinking. Beware of negative feeling. Spot it. Diagnose it. And deal with it. We have the power to transcend any situation and replace negative emotions with positive feelings, helping everyone else involved to do the same by engaging them anew in a positive process of success. The results can be striking.

ENTHUSIASM AT WORK

A man without a smiling face must not open a shop.

Chinese Proverb

People are attracted to people who care. This seems to be a universal law of human psychology. If we are enthusiastic about our work, other people will be attracted to join in and help us take that work to the next level. Nothing worth doing can be done alone. We need other people, and they need us. If we show enthusiasm for what we're doing day to day, others will be drawn to our enterprises.

No one wants to be around a grump. We all crave positive energy, exuberance, joy, the pure love of life, and when we see it in another person, we want to be around him or her. When people see it in us, they'll want to be around us as well.

The only reason they come to see me is that
I know life is great—and they know I know it.

Clark Gable (1901–1960)

In addition to its attractive energy, enthusiasm has another quality. It can be extremely contagious. All the greatest thinkers have noticed that we become like the people we're around. In the animal kingdom, it's known as imprinting. A baby duck picks up how to act from the big ducks, a puppy from a bigger dog. The same thing goes on in human life. The more attractive a person is, the more likely others are to imprint off that individual. And enthusiasm of the right sort can make anyone more attractive. The energy of the universe glows through him or her.

In a business context, nothing could be more important. One properly enthusiastic person on a team can ignite other members to a warmer glow of emotional energy. Two can set a team on fire.

Gloom can be a bit contagious too. But people resist gloom. Everybody deep down wants to be committed to something. So a properly displayed enthusiasm is one of the most attractive and infectious characteristics imaginable.

Nothing is so contagious as enthusiasm.
Samuel Taylor Coleridge (1772–1834)

Enthusiasm can become a habit, like almost anything else. I am an enthusiast about nearly everything I do. If I find a product I like, or a store, I become enthusiastic about that too. When I started writing with fountain pens several years ago, I preached the virtues of the well-drawn line to anyone who would listen. I penned a joyful celebration of the nib for *The Chicago Tribune.* I showed everyone I could my growing collection. And something interesting started to happen. Students and colleagues began buying fountain pens, and writing me notes with codicils like "Written with a beautiful blue Waterman fountain pen," or "Put onto paper with a burgundy Montblanc." My passion had communicated itself to others, who were then going out and spending hundreds of dollars on what had generated my enthusiasm.

The same thing happened every semester in the classroom during my years of teaching at Notre Dame. I was always charged up emotionally about the importance of what I taught. At the end of any given semester, an extraordinary number of students would tell me on evaluation forms how much they loved my class because of my enthusiasm. I even had students say to me, "Thank you for showing me that an adult can actually love what he's doing." But this perplexed me. Why weren't they seeing that everywhere in their lives? More of us need to live and display a passion about what we do. Many of the students who saw my emotional commitment to philosophy and to them have gone on to be people of great enthusiasm about whatever they have chosen to do in life. And they have gone on to success.

Enthusiasm is attractive. Enthusiasm is contagious. And a third benefit is just as important. Enthusiasm gives us an immediate point of contact with people of great accomplishment who, because of it, will see in us something of themselves.

Enthusiasts soon understand each other.
Washington Irving

Jack Welch, former CEO of General Electric, has been described as having 2,000 percent more energy than most people. On the one occasion I had the chance to meet and speak with him, I could see it, and I identified with it right away. But a further point is relevant here. Jack Welch didn't come at me like a steamroller, crushing me with an onrushing force of energy. He was an extraordinarily pleasant and gracious man, whose attractive energy shone through his face, words, and movements, without in the least seeming to overwhelm or appear in any way inappropriate in the relaxed social context in which we met.

Before I had ever seen him in person, the television producer Norman Lear had been described to me in a similar way as having "the energy of twelve people." On our first meeting, which turned into a five- or six-hour conversation on the front porch of his vacation house with a few other energetic high achievers, I saw it in the same way. We're not talking here about raving lunatics. We're talking about the most successful people in the world, and about a quality thoroughly compatible with a deep rationality and sensitivity to others. Enthusiasts do understand each other. And since we tend to work with people we understand, enthusiasts throughout the world tend to work with each other, at the highest levels of every enterprise. It's a very good thing to be an enthusiast.

If you're ever troubled by a lack of this emotional commitment, remind yourself of the elements for its genesis: First, you must be interested in what you're doing. Fascination is best. If you don't have it, do what it takes to get it. Second, you need desire for what you're pursuing. If the old pursuit has run out of steam, you need a new pursuit right away, within the job, attached to the job, or if all that is really impossible, and you know you've tried your best, then in a new job.

Third, you can overcome any emotional blockages to enthusiasm by transcending the negative and imaginatively nurturing the positive.

You can't sweep other people off their feet
if you can't be swept off your own.
Clarence Day (1874–1935)

Give yourself a Big Picture for what you're doing, find something to love about the job, and cultivate that love. Set goals whose attainment you can deeply desire, and when you achieve them, renew your vision. Chart out a strategy for pursuing your goals, launch out, keep your head up, stay on course, and indulge yourself in a little passion—or preferably, a lot. Then ride the biggest wave of enthusiasm you can to where you really belong. You deserve nothing less.

In all the sweep of human history, the most accomplished practitioners in every field of endeavor have tended to be people who genuinely loved what they were doing. Read the biographies of stellar achievers in business, science, politics, or the arts. You'll find stories of great passion behind those accounts of tremendous success.

Whenever I've come across someone whose quality of work I've admired as outstanding and I have had the chance to ask how they became so good, the answer inevitably has been "I love what I do." This connection between love and achievement has been recognized for a long time. In his *Symposium,* the great philosopher Plato has several characters at a dinner party speak eloquently on the topic of what love is and how it affects our experience of life. Referring to love as a divinity, the character Agathon praises the creative role of love in many domains of life, and at one point says, "Finally, in the production of craftsmanship, we know well that the man who has this god for his teacher turns out notable and famous, whereas the man who is untouched by Love remains obscure." Love, in this view, can make all the difference between remarkable achievement and obscurity. Talent alone can't do it. Neither can knowledge or hard work alone. There must be an extra spark that can come only from deep within our hearts.

In that same Platonic dialogue, the character Phaedrus says, "The principle which ought to guide the whole life of those who intend to live nobly cannot be implanted either by family or by position or by wealth or by anything else so effectively as by love." The greatest source of motivation on earth is internal and can arise only within our own souls. It is love, the ultimate form of emotional commitment. The art of emotional commitment is then just a form of the art of love.

To business that we love we rise betime
And go to't with delight
William Shakespeare (1564–1616)

It's only when we love and truly delight in what we're doing that we stand any good chance of delighting others with it over the long run. The art of commitment is a powerful art of delight.

PART 6

THE ART OF CHARACTER

We have too many high sounding words,
and too few actions that correspond with them.

Abigail Adams (1744–1818)

CHAPTER

Ethics and Success

16

CONDITION 6 OF THE 7 CS:
*We need a good **Character** to guide us and keep us on a proper course.*

Goodness is the only investment that never fails.
Henry David Thoreau

In my favorite movies through the years, the good guy has always won. It might not happen until the last possible minute, and things may have looked pretty bad up until then, but somehow you knew it was coming. From the early heroes of film to Luke Skywalker, Indiana Jones, and beyond, the good could be relied on to prevail. So why do we have the famous saying "Nice guys finish last"? Sure, we have it because Leo Durocher once said it and got quoted. But why did this remark become so well known?

The cynical among us might suggest that the reason this saying is so popular is, simply, that it's true. Nice guys are doomed. Billy Joel once went so far as to sing, "Only the good die young." But he wasn't the first. Wordsworth long ago penned the phrase "The good die first." It's no recent opinion.

Didn't the psalmist complain about this very thing long ago? "O God, why do the righteous suffer and the wicked prosper? O Lord, why do nice guys finish last? Lay waste the evil man, O God, blow him away. Send in Bruce Willis, Schwarzenegger, and Stallone, or maybe Pierce Brosnan could get the job done." Okay, I'm paraphrasing a bit. But read the Psalms. After a few pages, you can imagine God responding, "Complain, complain! Get over it, already!"

It has been recognized since ancient times that bad guys often win battles. And so we might conclude that we don't need some special explanation for the old saying about where nice guys finish. What you see is what you get. Perhaps what we do need is an account of why it so often goes the other way in books and movies.

Our cynic might go on to suggest that the reason we have heroic, triumphant good guys in film and fiction is because that's exactly what it is—fiction. We can't stand the fact that goodness gets stomped flat in the real world, and so we demand some satisfaction at least on the big screen and small page. We good guys get our vicarious revenge for what we put up with in the rough and tumble of our daily lives, doing business in this world, by watching goodness prevail in the only place where it has a chance, in the art of our collective fantasies.

Bull. The psalmist calms down a little bit in round thirty-seven, and gives us some words of great insight:

Do not fret because of evil men
or be envious of those who do wrong;
for like the grass they will soon wither,
like green plants they will soon die away.
Trust in the Lord and do good;
dwell in the land and enjoy safe pasture.
Delight yourself in the Lord
And he will give you the desires of your heart.
Psalm 37:1–4

The real reason that we have the heroic victory of good over evil in our greatest art and in our most satisfying forms of entertainment is that, despite many temporary indications to the contrary, deep down most of us feel that things will ultimately turn out this way, with the good guy ahead. Ultimately. But we like to see it within a two-hour span, which we don't often get to experience outside the cineplex. We have the cynical slogan "Nice guys finish last" just because we have cynics, and because even the best of us can sometimes have our doubts. But the wisest thinkers have always seen that good character is a precondition for true and lasting success.

Remember, the kind of achievement I'm talking about is deeply satisfying success that's sustainable over the long run. That's how I can claim that character is one of The 7 Cs of Success, a universal condition of altogether positive, lasting attainment. It's also my suggestion that there is an art of character that is one of the most ancient arts of achievement, an ethical way of working and living that can make a big difference in our long-term prospects.

The integrity of the upright guides them,
but the crookedness of the treacherous destroys them.
Proverbs 11:3

There is no doubt that a bad character can have striking success—for a while, and in a limited domain. But unethical achievement is always purchased at great expense, at the cost of everything that really matters, and unethical accomplishment is, in the long run, what is really doomed in our world. That's what will wither. The psalmist eventually got it right.

When we plug into the positive energy of the universe, we experience delight. We can attain the kind of success that will satisfy our hearts with enduring benefit. What perplexed the psalmist at times was not that evil always prevails. It doesn't, not now and not then. What puzzled the ancient writer was, first, that evil ever triumphs at all and, second, that it does do so with irritating frequency, however temporary its victory might be.

Our newspapers bring us plenty of accounts of the temporary ascendancy of evil, greed, and selfishness. But the stories usually get written only when something has gone wrong, or, perhaps, right, and the party's over. The house of financial cards comes tumbling down, and we see the former world-beater morosely shuffling off, handcuffed, into court. Or, sometimes, worse.

Unethical practices always carry within themselves the seeds of their own destruction. Only business based on ethical practices, relationships founded on what the ancients identified as virtue, and a self-development of good character will endure and flourish throughout all the dimensions of our lives.

The glory that goes with wealth and beauty is fleeting and fragile;
virtue is a possession glorious and eternal.
Sallust

REFLECTED ACTION

Unethical conduct is self-defeating over the long haul, no matter how effective it might seem in the short run. One reason we have had so many ethical problems in modern business is that we have had too many short-term thinkers calling the shots. We need a big-picture perspective for our enterprises, as well as for our lives, in order to see the most important consequences of our actions.

Some reflection on the basic principles of human action will help us see what we need to appreciate in order to appraise our actions accurately and understand the importance of ethical conduct. We can make a good start by peering into the core of ethics.

There is one ethical rule recognized in some form by every advanced civilization. It can be understood as the key to living and working with other people. It has been thought of as the most important ethical rule ever articulated. It has even been described as the heart of morality. We know it as the Golden Rule. Before we go on, banish from your mind the cynic's version: "He who has the gold makes the rules." This is nothing more than another form of the famous saying "Might makes right," which, for all its catchiness, has never been even remotely right.

Thence arises that Golden Rule of dealing with others
as we would have others deal with us.
Izaak Walton (1593–1683)

Let me give you just a few examples of the various statements of the Golden Rule made throughout history:

Confucianism: "Do not do unto others what you would not want them to do unto you."
Buddhism: "Seek for others the happiness you desire for yourself. Hurt not others with that which pains you."
Judaism: "That which is hurtful to you, do not do to your fellow man."
Islam: "Let none of you treat his brother in a way he himself would not like to be treated. No one of you is a believer until he loves for his brother what he loves for himself."
Taoism: "View your neighbor's gain as your own gain, and your neighbor's loss as your own loss."

In American culture, we are perhaps most familiar with the Christian version, "Do unto others as you would have them do unto you," or "Treat others as you would want to be treated."

Moral leaders seek to live the by Golden Rule. Many of us believe it describes our practice. But the unfortunate truth is that most people seem to live by another principle altogether, one that I often call the Rule of Reciprocity, because it involves just reciprocating the sort of conduct we receive: "Do unto others as they do unto you," or "Treat others the way you are treated." If I'm living reciprocally, then I'll treat you well if you've treated me well, but I'll treat you badly if you've done so to me.

Look around. Don't most people seem to live much of the time like mirrors? If they're treated rudely, they reply brusquely. If they're dealt with nicely, they're basically polite in turn.

One problem with the Rule of Reciprocity is that when you live by it you allow others to call the shots. You become reactive rather than setting the tone of action yourself. You act as a moral puppet, which is not a high form of human dignity. But, like it or not, we deal with people every day who fall into this pattern of conduct and just reflect back to us whatever we do to them.

This is a truth of great importance, since it gives us one of the main reasons why unethical business practices are self-destructive. It may be easy to treat people badly one by one, or a few at a time, but over the long run, if you have treated enough other people terribly, and they are living reciprocally, then they are out there as a growing multitude preparing to do the same to you. And together, they'll eventually have the power to bring you down.

You must expect to be treated by others
as you have treated them.

Seneca

It was as true in the first century as it is now. By treating others badly, you set yourself up for bad times. By treating others well, you pave the way for your own success. In particular, if you treat other people in accordance with the Golden Rule, and they are acting on nothing more than reciprocity, then you make it more and more difficult for them to refrain from so treating you. And, if I may second an opinion once expressed by Socrates, I'd prefer to make the people around me better than to make them worse. It's the only sensible course. We reap what we sow.

We are paid in our own coin.

Pliny the Younger (ca. 61–113)

It has been said that "The Golden Rule works like gravity." If this is true, it is not because the Golden Rule pulls us down and holds our feet to the ground, but rather because it draws other people to us in a positive way, it is as inexorable as the most basic laws of nature, and the good it does, it accomplishes with as much exceptionless necessity as that most obvious of laws from whose governance none can escape. With its help we truly rise up and fly.

TRUTH AND TRUST

Ethical practices engaged in consistently produce the conditions for trust, and trust may be the most important factor there is for long-term business and personal success. In particular, nothing else produces trust like action in accordance with the Golden Rule.

People will not willingly engage their deepest talents and take new personal risks to help us unless they trust us. They won't stick with us in tough times unless they feel well treated by us. By acting on the basis of simple, straightforward moral principles like the Golden Rule, and by showing in our actions the basic moral virtues like truthfulness, justice, and kindness, we build the foundation for successful relationships and enduring joint endeavors with others.

It is better to trust virtue than fortune.

Publilius Syrus

My friend Ken Schanzer was a vice president of NBC Sports, and was considered to be next in line for president, a job he eagerly anticipated. On the day the new president was to be named, the network announced that it would be Dick Ebersol, a very accomplished individual at NBC who had not previously been a part of the sports division. As the newly appointed leader made the rounds to meet all the sports executives who now would be reporting to him, he was greeted by a sea of smiles, good wishes, and hearty congratulations all around. But when he went into Schanzer's office, he experienced something very different.

"I'm the most disappointed I've ever been in my life," Schanzer stated point-blank. No one else had expressed any hint of a negative sentiment to Ebersol, despite his being an outsider suddenly brought in to run the sports enterprise over all the seasoned insiders who had expected one of their own to ascend to the job. Schanzer spoke to him with complete candor. "But I understand how this can be a good thing for NBC Sports," he continued, and then went on to list the strengths Ebersol could bring to the position. He concluded by saying, "I'll do everything I can to help you do the job well."

We must not always say everything,
for that would be folly;
but what we say must be what we think.
Montaigne

Few people expected an individual in Schanzer's position to stay on in the division after something like this. But he did. And that honest conversation launched a relationship between the two men that has come to be a centerpiece in both their personal and professional lives. Schanzer, who is now president of NBC Sports, recently told me that what had seemed at the time to be the worst day of his life had become instead one of the best days ever. Every good thing in his career after that day came out of the relationship that grew from those first seeds of honesty. Ebersol sensed he could trust Schanzer. And Schanzer soon felt the same about Ebersol.

He who wishes to secure the good of others
has already secured his own.
Confucius

"Guys at the top are brutally honest with each other," Schanzer recently told me. The best leaders don't have time for elaborate games with truth and falsehood. They need truth to steer by. Trust is necessary. Character counts. A strong character is indeed the foundation for great relationships. And relationships rule the world.

The best leaders treat their associates with respect. In little details as well as in big things, the way we treat others affects profoundly how they will respond, both to us and to our goals. Because of that, I've come to believe that etiquette is a broad domain of human behavior where ethics meets everyday life. Manners are morals in action. The respect and dignity that we accord others in little ways, day to day, makes all the difference in the world to what we can do together. In most areas of human endeavor, the most accomplished people tend to be individuals who treat others well, and who can, as a result, depend on their goodwill as a resource for moving into the future together.

Politeness is to human nature what warmth is to wax.
Arthur Schopenhauer

Nothing of great worth can ever be done by one person completely alone. Human achievements are meant to be social. It's of vital importance to build good relationships on a foundation of good conduct if our aim is to see great long-term results from our actions. Ethical behavior is crucial for true success in any endeavor involving other people.

So, do nice guys finish last? I think it's more likely that nice guys actually finish. And that nice guys last.

CHAPTER

17 The Business of Character

As we are, so we do;
and as we do, so is it done to us.
Ralph Waldo Emerson

In almost every business, ethics has increasingly come to be a topic of discussion. But far too often, ethics is misunderstood in this context as being nothing more than a matter of sometimes complex rules and scrupulously documented compliance with them. The truth is simpler, and much more powerful.

Business ethics is all about character and culture—individual character and corporate culture. But then, what we refer to as corporate culture is just the character of the organization. So business ethics is, at its core, always a matter of character. In one way or another, all of ethics revolves around this issue. So it's no coincidence that character is one of The 7 Cs of Success.

Ethics is often thought of as focusing on what we do. But character is a matter of who we are. It's the relationship between the two that we need to look at just a bit.

Character is a starting point. It launches action. But it's also a result. Our actions affect it and build it. And they also affect others, who then act and affect us. To grasp what it takes for lasting success along the ethical dimension, we need to understand this process.

THE DYNAMIC OF CHARACTER

What do we mean when we speak of "character" and "good character"? A person's moral character is, paradoxically, both the source and the result of his or her actions.

First, it is the source. Emerson was right when he said, "As we are, so we do." Our character is the sum total of morally what we are—our inclinations, tendencies, dispositions, and patterns of desire and intention. It is the basis for our responses to the world, and is the fountain of our initiatives as well. It determines what we are most likely to do, and who we are most likely to become.

By knowing something of our character, other people have reasonable expectations concerning how we are likely to act and react in various situations. We say of a person who is good at sizing up others, "He is a good judge of character." A person who can see into the realities of character can discern the possibilities and likelihoods of the future.

His own character is the arbiter of every man's fortune.

Publilius Syrus

We can't get oranges from an apple tree. We don't get energetic initiative or reliable follow-through from a slacker. Honorable deeds don't come from a corrupt man. And that's one reason a friend of mine, when assessing possible business partners, likes to say, "You can't make a good deal with a bad man." No matter how good the deal looks, if it's with a person who has a bad character, the whole thing is bound to turn bad sooner or later.

We won't likely get the results we want in our lives unless we are operating on the basis of good character. We won't tend to produce good consequences over the long run if we're working with bad people.

A man's character is his guardian divinity.

Heraclitus

The core defense of any business against everything that might assail it is the character of the people who do the work. That's the core strength of any cooperative endeavor. We all need to ask ourselves what the character of our workplace is. What qualities are we encouraging in our day-to-day activities at work? Are these the characteristics that will give rise to long-term good? Is truthfulness encouraged? Is trust cultivated? Do we look out for each other and the overall good? Are we in the habit of thinking of our customers' needs just as we think of our own? How do we habitually react to frustrations or unexpected problems? Are we positive problem solvers? Do we transcend the immediacy of an irritation and move forward in a constructive way? Do we show respect for all our coworkers? These are questions of character. Who we are, the character we have, will generate what we do and what we become.

Character isn't inherited.
One builds it daily by the way one thinks and acts,
thought by thought, action by action.
If one lets fear or hate or anger take possession of the mind,
they become self-forged chains.

Helen Gahagan Douglas (1900–1980)

Character is a source, but it's also, and very importantly, a result. Aristotle stressed that human beings are always in a state of becoming. What we are becoming is determined largely by what we are doing day after day. In a recent book called *Leadership Is an Art,* Max Depree, the former Herman Miller CEO, pointed out that every company is always in a state of becoming, dependent on what the people who work there are individually, and together, becoming. In charting out our strategic directions, and in solving everyday problems, we ought always to be asking ourselves: "In doing this, are we becoming the kind of company we really want to be?" and "In consenting to this, or in recommending this, will I be moving in the direction of becoming the kind of person I really want to be?"

Every man is the son of his own works.

Miguel de Cervantes

One of the most dangerous assumptions in life is that we can isolate our actions and their effects. Suppose you're confronting a difficult problem and it seems to you that the quickest solution would involve doing something you normally wouldn't do or even approve of doing. But this one time, you think to yourself, it doesn't make sense to play by the rules, or we really don't have time to do anything else than cut a few corners, but nobody's going to know, and it's just one situation, not a new policy.

I hope that if you're ever tempted to think like this, the moral equivalent of warning lights and buzzers go off in your head so loud you have to sit down, get a grip, and start over. Everything we do sets up patterns of tendency, proclivities of future thought and action. Every single decision, however small, has internal repercussions in our characters. There are no exceptions.

There is nothing insignificant.
Samuel Taylor Coleridge

Every action plants a seed. Every decision makes us a little more likely to decide in a similar way again. How we choose and how we act affects even how we perceive our circumstances. Having thought about one situation in a way that you're morally unaccustomed to thinking sets you up to perceive the next situation that you'll confront in a similar way. If we begin to depart from a reliable moral framework in our dealings with others, we begin to attend to different features of our experience, different aspects of the world around us. It's sometimes very subtle, but that makes it tremendously insidious. Actions and tendencies set up habits of mind, and habits soon become something more than what they are in themselves—they become part of us. Continued long enough, they become aspects of our moral character.

Character is simply habit long continued.
Plutarch

Everyone's character is composed of habits of mind as well as habits of action. This is one of the most overlooked aspects of ethics in the modern world, and it's one of the most important.

How do you habitually think about your work? How do you think about the people who work with you? About your clients, your customers? What do you pay attention to? Most of us think of ethics and character as having to do primarily with our actions, with what we decide, and what we actually do. The late British philosopher Iris Murdoch had a different opinion, which I want to quote in some detail. She thought of character and what she called "the moral life" as having to do mainly with attention. What do we attend to throughout the day? What we focus our attention on has been a major concern of all the world's great religious traditions. And there is a powerful reason for this. In her little book *The Sovereignty of Good,* Murdoch offered an interesting insight while discussing the nature of moral decision making. She wrote:

> But if we consider what the work of attention is like, how continuously it goes on, and how imperceptibly it builds up structures of value round about us, we shall not be surprised that at crucial moments of choice most of the business of choosing is already over.
>
> The moral life, on this view, is something that goes on continually, not something that is switched off in between the occurrence of explicit moral choices. What happens in between such choices is indeed what is crucial.

What do we attend to in the course of a normal business day? What do we think about and talk about? We think business. We think market share. We attend to inventory and orders. We focus on product development. We have our minds on the competition. We worry about customer service and customer problems. We fret over the report that's due. We rehash the big meeting. We fixate on a new technology. We talk numbers.

I've been told repeatedly by honorable people, working in companies with publicly high ethical standards, that they rarely if ever have conversations at work about ethical issues, about company character, or about the moral nature of their relations with suppliers and clients. Apart from the occasional ethical brush fire, values and morals hardly ever enter their thoughts during the business day. Is this because character issues are unimportant? Do they somehow take care of themselves? Are ethical issues normally out of place at work? No. It's just that the tyranny of the trivial but urgent often crowds out the more subtly and deeply important things in life.

We generally do not attend to the ethical side of our endeavors until there is a sudden problem dropped in our laps, and then we most often try desperately to create solutions from scratch. We then sometimes discover that we don't have the habits of thought and attention required for solving moral problems in a natural and deeply appropriate way or, better yet, for avoiding as many of them as possible in the first place.

In business schools and management books, everyone has been talking for years about "the learning organization." We continue to multiply our information-gathering competencies like never before in human history, but with all this new technical, financial, and organizational knowledge at our disposal, are we also cultivating the individual and corporate character to use what we know properly? Too often, the answer is simply: No. And this is quite dangerous.

Integrity without knowledge is weak and useless,
and knowledge without integrity is dangerous and dreadful.
Samuel Johnson

In this life, we are either growing or deteriorating. We are being built up, or we are being torn down. It's of the utmost importance that we take care about which process we are engaged in. It can be a real challenge to build strong character. But it's even a greater challenge to rehabilitate a character that has been diminished and overcome the many negative results of neglect.

Character is much easier kept than recovered.
Thomas Paine (1737–1809)

It makes little difference what we know if we haven't attended to who we are. Value considerations need to take their rightful place at the conference table on a regular basis. We need to be more continually attuned to character issues and how they interplay with the challenges we face on a daily basis. As hard as it is to build positive character in a company, or in our own souls, it is much easier to create and push forward a positive momentum than to resuscitate and reverse the trend of a fading ethical sensibility.

INTEGRITY

Whenever issues of character and ethics are being discussed, one word that often comes up is "integrity." Morally good people are proud of their integrity. Businesses with foresight insist on it in their employees. Hardly any moral word is more familiar in the modern marketplace. But what exactly is this prized quality of integrity?

The etymology of the word is telling. Think of our word "integer," which means "whole number." "Integration" brings our whole population together in classrooms, neighborhoods, and businesses. An "integral" part of something contributes to a greater whole, or a more complex unity.

Integrity is a kind of moral wholeness, or ethical unity. Do we always bring the entirety, or wholeness, of who we are and what we stand for to our decisions? If we leave aside some of our principles or values when they're difficult or inconvenient to put into action, then we're not making a decision with integrity. Is there a wholeness to our actions through time? Is there a value consistency, or moral unity, to what we do? Are our actions and words at one with the deepest moral principles there are? That's integrity. That's the quality crucial for good character.

A little integrity is better than any career.
Ralph Waldo Emerson

Chris Spielman was living the adventure of his dreams as an NFL linebacker. A high school All-America, he had his picture on a Wheaties box at the age of seventeen. After he had played for Ohio State in the Rose Bowl and Cotton Bowl, the Detroit Lions launched him into professional football, where he broke records for tackling. When he moved on to Buffalo, the owner of the Buffalo Bills once said, "He is the most intense player we've had here in thirty-seven years."

This was a man who loved football. He had an emotional commitment that could not be beat. He thanked God every day that he was an NFL player. But when his wife, Stefanie, was diagnosed with a serious case of breast cancer, he immediately quit the game to stay home and take care of her. He said it was "a nondecision." No deliberation was needed. He just brought the wholeness of his values to the situation and did what he knew was right.

Nothing but your best is good enough.
Elbert Hubbard

Integrity means never bringing less than your whole self into a situation. Chris attacked the challenge of his wife's cancer with the same focus that had served him so well in football. When she started losing her hair as a result of chemotherapy, he shaved his head as well. The difficult new adventure they had been thrust into proceeded with pain, determination, solidarity, and hope. And Stephanie got better.

Full effort is full victory.
Mohandas Gandhi (1869–1948)

When Chris finally returned to football, it was only because of restored health in both their lives. He had been injured the previous year, with a ruptured disc, and after a tough rehabilitation, had just been ready to play again when his wife's cancer was discovered. Now, with both of them healthy once more, he was eager to resume his old job. But in an early game, a strong hit produced a temporary paralysis in his arms and legs that alarmed team doctors. If he continued to play he would run a high risk of being permanently paralyzed. Once again, his sense of duty to himself, his wife, and his children helped Chris Spielman to close the book on his incredible athletic career and move on to the next stage of his personal journey. If he brings the same conditions of success into the new adventures that lie ahead for him, I have no doubt about the impact he can continue to have.

Integrity and firmness are all I can promise.
These, be the voyage long or short, shall never forsake me,
although I may be deserted by all men; for of the consolations,
which are to be derived from these, under any circumstances,
the world cannot deprive me.
George Washington (1732–1799)

Personal integrity can be the compass by which we steer our lives and govern our emotions. It can help us keep our bearings in times of excitement as well as hardship, and help give us a sense of direction at each step along the way. A person operating from the deepest resources of integrity will understand which adventures in life are appropriate and which should be left alone.

A person of integrity is trusted by others because they know they can count on him. He's reliable. He operates from a core of values that doesn't fluctuate. He stands on principle not just when it's convenient, but whenever it's right. Integrity is a condition for sustainable success, for both individuals and organizations.

Integrity is one of the most important components of truly good character. The other components would include all the specific virtues—such qualities as honesty, courage, kindness, fairness, and humility. Too many companies try to legislate all of ethics in complex lists of rules. Rules are important to generate and ground mutual expectations in any business or profession, but rules alone can never cover the whole territory of ethics. Rules can never capture the full richness of good character. Ethics, ultimately, is an art. Character is an art. It's not a science. There never can be a complete set of guidelines that automatically will tell us what to do in all possible situations. The best way to learn ethical decision making, the application of integrity, is by modeling ourselves on good people who are farther along life's road than we are. Then we too can become artists of the ethical whom others can emulate as well.

They're only truly great who are truly good.
George Chapman (ca. 1559–1634)

People in positions of authority in any business need to look for the qualities of good character when hiring, and then nurture those qualities as they guide, assign, and promote. If integrity and other matters of character are not perceived as entering into a company's system of rewards and incentives, that company will not develop or sustain the kind of character necessary for long-term world-class achievement. The art of character needs patrons in high places. It needs modeling. And it needs encouragement.

Socrates once said that it's a bad thing to suffer evil, but a much worse thing to do it. An evil action harms not only the obvious victim, but also the doer of the deed. Socrates also pointed out that others can damage our bodies, but only we can harm our souls. If we are on a journey of true success, that's a form of damage we need to avoid. For, as this great thinker also believed, the health of the soul is the deepest foundation for sustainable, satisfying success there is.

PART 7

THE ART OF CAPACIOUS ENJOYMENT

Art comes to you proposing frankly
to give nothing but the highest quality
to your moments as they pass.

Walter Pater (1839–1894)

CHAPTER

18 The Joy of the Journey

CONDITION 7 OF THE 7 Cs:

We need a ***Capacity to Enjoy*** *the process along the way.*

If you are practicing the first six arts of success, and have the first six of The 7 Cs of Success working for you, then you're providing yourself with everything that is within your power for a joyous personal journey, an adventure of growth and fulfilling accomplishment that can be relished with every fiber of your being. The seventh condition says: "So, enjoy it!" The art of enjoyment is a vital practice for any ongoing experience of sustainable and satisfying achievement.

We could hardly wait to get up in the morning!

Wilbur and Orville Wright (1867–1912; 1871–1948)

It's easy to see the many relationships between the seventh condition of success and the others. A person of good character isn't always looking over her shoulder, worried about being found out or anticipating the retaliations of people who feel wronged by her actions. Strength of character can enhance immensely our capacity to enjoy the process, whatever adventure we're on. An enthusiastic emotional commitment can certainly facilitate enjoyment as well. And the same goes for each of the other conditions.

Conversely, the seventh condition makes the others easier. People who love and enjoy what they're doing are in the best possible inner state for creative goal setting. Stressed-out, miserable people don't tend to be masterful goal setters. People who enjoy their work are also apt to be more confident in it. It's easier to be consistent when you like what you're doing. And so on.

My wife, Mary, has two little tricks for enjoying tasks that are not intrinsically pleasant, like pruning the shrubs around our house. First, she uses an ancient strategy for dealing with any difficult problem: Divide, then conquer. She focuses her concentration on, say, three shrubs, and her vision for how they should look. Then she starts with one, and gets it perfect—an artistic masterpiece. She allows herself a moment to just enjoy the look of that one botanical sculpture and feel good about what she's accomplished. Then she goes on to the next one, repeating the process. When her first three are all done, she attends to that result, enjoying this larger unit of aesthetic improvement, and she inwardly celebrates her achievement. The process can then begin again. Dividing and conquering, setting small goals, and relishing their attainment along the way is her path for mastering difficult, dreaded, and otherwise unenjoyable tasks.

It is the disposition of thought
which altereth the nature of the thing.
John Lyly (1554–1606)

The second trick my creative spouse uses is to put things mentally into a positive perspective. While working in the yard, she purposely resists recounting to herself how hot it is, how many bugs are around, or how much needs to be done. Instead, she tells herself that she's getting good exercise and saving money that she would have had to pay to have the work done by a professional. After receiving a particularly high estimate from a local landscaper for some gardening we needed done right away, she recently went into overdrive doing it herself, inwardly cheering herself on with reminders of all the money we weren't having to spend, and mentally deciding which of the shoes in the newest Saks catalog she'd order for herself as a little reward for all the cash she was saving.

There is no object on earth that cannot be
looked at from a cosmic point of view.
Fyodor Dostoyevsky

Mary also manages the financial affairs of both the Morris family and our newly founded Institute for Human Values, an arena that is much more intricately challenging and intrinsically unrewarding than even the toughest gardening. But she uses the same procedures here. A compound strategy like this can be employed in any job, and in almost any of life's circumstances. There is indeed an art of enjoyment, and it is often up to us to decide whether to practice it or not. When we divide our work into manageable tasks whose accomplishment can be enjoyed, and put things into the most positive perspective possible, even if that involves the Saks catalog, we position ourselves to enjoy the process in ways that otherwise might not have been possible.

I've become convinced that everything in life falls into one of two categories: It's either something we can enjoy, or else it's something we can learn from—and later we can enjoy having learned. Some things are just intrinsically enjoyable. Pleasure is good, although we don't often learn a lot from it. But some things are not pleasurable at all. There is nothing about them to enjoy. Maybe they involve extreme unpleasantness, or even tragedy and terrible suffering. In such situations, if we are philosophically grounded and sufficiently attentive, we can learn deeply. And then later, sometimes much later, we can appreciate, and even enjoy, the depth of feeling, along with the breadth of perspective and understanding, that our sufferings brought into our lives.

Whenever we can find a way to enjoy some aspect of the process of working toward a goal, we facilitate our success in attaining that goal. The more aspects of the process we can enjoy, the better. The art of enjoyment is truly an art of achievement. And as many philosophers, from the Stoics on, have taught us, it often just comes down to the mind game we choose to play with ourselves. Do we mentally endow a process with enjoyable aspects, or do we allow external circumstances and other people's attitudes to dictate our own inner states? To the extent that we inwardly take control of our feelings, attitudes, and emotional perspectives, we empower ourselves to have a better shot at success, whatever the adventure happens to be and whatever challenges it brings our way.

The test of a vocation is the love of the drudgery it involves.

Logan Pearsall Smith

LOVE IT OR LEAVE IT

Do you love your work? Do you feel it's worth doing? Do you think, in particular, that you should be doing it?

Do you work only for some external compensation, or do you enjoy the process along the way, the actual tasks you do each day, or at least most of what you do on most days? Even when it's hard, do you find something satisfying about a job well done? Without the right answers to these questions, you can't be sure that what you're doing is something at which you'll excel and contribute what you are here to give the world. With the right answers, you can know you're on your way.

It has been said often enough that success is a journey, not a destination. The work we do, as a path of success, is not meant to be painful drudgery, a grim guts-and-blood sacrifice of sheer self-discipline and nearly masochistic forced effort, endured for some far-off greater good. It's meant to involve enjoyment along the way. In fact, without a joy of some sort in the ordinary texture of what we're doing, we're not likely to be doing it with excellence.

I don't mean that work should never feel hard and involve unpleasant effort. We're sometimes in tough situations where the best way out is difficult. Everything worth doing is typically harder than we think. Every minute of every day can't be uninterrupted glee. We need to appreciate the occasional necessity of sheer self-discipline and uncomfortable struggle. But this should not be the norm, or the emotional bottom line. Even very demanding work should bring us something positive along the way.

In his book *Life Work,* the poet Donald Hall tells an interesting story about a novelist named Gurcharan Das, who was also a business executive, serving as CEO for Procter & Gamble in India. Das was addressing a working conference of four hundred young managers in Bombay. In their Q&A session, one man raised his hand and, displaying the uncanny Indian proclivity for raising philosophical issues in almost any context, asked suddenly, "What is contentment?"

Hall comments: "If an American junior executive asked such a question in public, would he remain a junior executive?" We might at least wonder whether in some companies he would risk becoming even more junior.

Das told the group that he needed two minutes before he would be able to answer the question. They waited. He then stated his opinion that contentment is "absorbedness."

Hall adds to this his own view that contentment is "work so engrossing that you do not know that you are working." He then later goes on to say about his own work as a writer, "In the best part of the best day, *absorbedness* occupies me from footsole to skulltop." Absorbedness.

"What is work?" and "What is not work?"
are questions that perplex the wisest of men.
The Bhagavad Gita

Are you absorbed? Are the people around you absorbed? Do you, and they, have work to do that can create a feeling of total immersion? Can you become so involved that you forget you're working? Do you ever have the feeling that you'd enjoy what you're doing even if you didn't get paid for it? Are there at least some aspects of your job like that?

A proper path of success is absorbing. It is engrossing. It demands and rewards. It catches us up into something greater than just ourselves. It's never just about doing or getting. It's always about serving and becoming.

Do you and the people who work with you have something important to believe in connected to the work you do? Is it challenging, yet manageable? Does it generate personal growth? Does it both do good and feel good? How often does it seem really satisfying? How often do you feel happy, both in what you're doing and about what you're doing?

Growth itself contains the germ of happiness.
Pearl S. Buck (1892–1973)

If your honest answers to these questions are fairly negative, then you need to make a change. It's time for a change in what you do, or in how you approach it. You may need a little vacation, a change of pace, or no pace at all, for a least a while. You may just need some refreshment and rejuvenation. Perhaps you can mentally reframe your work, thinking of it in a fresh way that inspires new love for the job. Or you may need to make a bigger adjustment. You may be getting a signal from your unconscious that the time has come for a different adventure, either within the context of your present work, or in a new context altogether.

The ant is knowing and wise;
but he doesn't know enough to take a vacation.
Clarence Day

We human beings are not ants with intricately complex, organically installed software programs that run from birth to death, keeping us in the same array of activities over and over and over again. We are vastly more complex souls, growing and changing as we do what we do, and as we daily and hourly experience what crosses our paths. What was right for us yesterday may not be right for us tomorrow, or the day after that.

We all need to take time periodically to reflect on our lives and determine whether we are living a satisfying, fulfilling adventure or not. Socrates said that the unexamined life is not worth living. The unexamined life is at least not likely to lead to deep fulfillment. Sometimes we need to step off the treadmill for a bit just to think it all over and reexamine how we're using our time and energies.

Commitment is important in human life, as is perseverance. But adaptability is equally important. It's often a difficult but necessary exercise in self-knowledge to come to know when and how to make a change. My father's advice has stayed with me for decades. He would say to me, "As long as you enjoy what you're doing and think you have something distinctive to contribute, stick with it. But if either of those things changes, you make a change."

We should all do what,
in the long run, gives us joy,
even if it is only picking grapes or sorting the laundry.
E. B. White (1899–1985)

We are here to discover our talents, develop those talents, and deploy them into the world for the good of others as well as ourselves. Each one of us is intended to experience our own forms of excellence and achievement. We're also meant to find enjoyment in what we do. If your joy is gone and you can't bring it back, if new approaches to your work don't bring any sense of satisfaction, then you may need to make a more radical change. Your work as an artist of enjoyment may require it. But again, external changes rarely solve internal problems, so I always caution people about jumping ship before doing all they can to reenergize their present circumstances. Enjoyment is ultimately up to us.

Pam Kersting worked in sales for two of the top textbook publishers in America before taking a similar job in the world of computers. After a time, she came to realize she was not enjoying her work. Instead, it provoked overwhelming anxiety and didn't bring any compensating sense of fulfillment. What was great for others wasn't right for her. She gradually began to understand that her work needed to mean more to her, with her specific talents and interests. She decided it was time for a change, and entered into a period of self-discovery launched by a simple question: "What makes me happy?"

Answering that question launched a career change that made all the difference in the world. Pam is now a successful landscape architect who loves her work "a million times more" than anything she ever did before. I have seen her perform magic, transforming a barren plot of dirt into a beautiful garden. Her joy in her job manifests itself in a remarkable excellence of accomplishment. I recently asked her what she enjoys most about her work. She told me first of the great feeling she has in "taking nothing and making it something." She spoke of the sense of fulfillment that comes from helping make other people's dreams come true. She concluded by saying, "What I love most about it is that I'm learning something every day."

The important point is this:
to be able at any moment to sacrifice what we are
for what we could become.
Charles Du Bos (1882–1939)

Love is always connected to learning. All of us can look back on the times in our lives where we have had the most intense enjoyment and see that they were times of great learning—learning a new sport, a new job, learning about a new person, or learning new things about a person already close to us. Love and learning go together. Typically, people lose their first love for what they're doing when they cease to learn in satisfying ways and fall into repetitious patterns of action. A love or enjoyment for your work often depends on rediscovering something satisfying to learn, whether a new aspect of the job you already have, or a new task altogether. What makes you happy? That simple question is a key to discovering what you should be doing.

If you want to make your mark in the world, you must follow your heart. A lack of love for what you're doing always signals the need for some sort of change, however subtle or radical. But here's a more surprising piece of news. Even if you already enjoy immensely what you now do, you may still find yourself at a juncture in your life, at some point, where you should move on to another stage in your personal adventure and an even greater enjoyment of the process of work.

A good thing which prevents us from
enjoying a greater good is in truth an evil.
Spinoza (1632–1677)

This is a hard truth to learn and accept. Most of us are so keen to find something enjoyable to do that when we first find such a task, we wouldn't think about ever leaving it for anything else. Sometimes we are right to be comfortable and stay in what we're already doing. As long as we are doing good, and continuing to grow, our comfort and love for our job may be a sign that it's well matched to our talents and tastes. But the danger is that our enjoyment of what we're doing can lure us into staying on a certain course beyond the time that is right for us in our overall personal growth. An equal or greater joy may await us elsewhere.

The message here is that enjoyment need not be the end of the road. Often, it can be a powerful beginning. An enjoyable job can be a path through life. Or it can be the base camp for your next ascent up the new peak that has just come into view. A deep enjoyment should be part of any life process in which we invest significant energy. But the fact that you enjoy one thing you're doing now should never in itself be a sufficient reason for you to cease to explore other possibilities. Life is meant to be a series of adventures. Whether they're external adventures, or matters of internal growth, we need to keep ourselves open to the next challenge.

CHILDLIKE PLAY

With enjoyment, the point is not to pursue it for its own sake, and to tread water when we have it, but to cultivate it in the pursuit of other things that are worth our time and energy. We can rediscover a childlike joy as we do very adult things.

A childlike man is not a man whose development has been arrested; on the contrary, he is a man who has given himself a chance of continuing to develop long after most adults have muffled themselves in the cocoon of middle-aged habit and convention.
Aldous Huxley (1894–1963)

Playful people are very often creative people. A joyous exuberance in learning and doing, along with a creative approach to life, can move anyone farther along the road of their own personal excellence, and can bring with it a satisfying sense of achievement.

To recapture a sense of play and the joy of the present moment, we need to renew in ourselves our inborn ability to embrace the moment and live in it. Nothing is more endangered in the modern world than the powerful combination of hard work toward meaningful goals joined with an exuberant embrace of the present moment. Nowadays, we seem to think you have to make a choice: You can be a present-embracer or you can be a goal-seeker. The prejudice here is that the goal-seeker is future directed, while the now-lover is blind to past and future, and is rather focused on seizing the day, this moment, and nothing else.

Nothing is worth more than this day.
Goethe

Goethe was right. He believed in the unparalleled value of the present moment. But he was a very accomplished person. He saw deeply, lived deeply, and, as a result, enjoyed immense success.

We don't have to choose between accomplishment and enjoyment. We can have both. We can be both teleological, purposive workers, throwing ourselves into meaningful challenges, and at the same time lovers of the present moment. In fact, I've come to believe that we can't be workers at the highest level of excellence, over the long run, unless we do find that joy in the process now, in a warm embrace of immediacy. Just as important, we can't fully relish any moment we live unless we have it and see it in a purposive overall context of creative work. It's a dynamic balance. Purpose and play can and must go together.

Think about each of the first six conditions and arts of success for a moment. Goal setting can be joyous. Confidence building can be fun. Focusing our concentration on every step it takes to reach our goals, we can feel deep fulfillment in the progress we are making. Living consistently can yield a gratifying sense of power. Emotional commitment can bring the highs of enthusiasm. Character can generate a feeling of satisfaction that nothing else can surpass.

The first six conditions of success and their related arts of achievement can provide the best possible framework for a meaningful and enduring enjoyment of life. The seventh condition urges us to act in such a way as to cultivate this last piece of the puzzle. The art of enjoyment awaits our initiative. It allows us to be complete in our quest.

CHAPTER

Meaning and Joy

19

In work, the greatest satisfaction lies—the satisfaction of stretching yourself, using your abilities and making them expand, and knowing that you have accomplished something that could have been done only by you using your unique apparatus. This is really the centre of life, and those who never orient themselves in this direction are missing more than they ever know.

Kenneth Alsop (1920–1973)

Where is enjoyment most to be found? In money? In fame? In the prestige of high social status? In being surrounded by great stuff? What's interesting is that it's frequently the people who have experienced the most of these widely sought quarries who say that, no, these are not the deepest sources of enjoyment in life at all.

Too often we chase things, thinking that they will make us happy. A certain kind of house in a particular neighborhood, a great car, a membership in a specific club, a vacation house in just the right spot, high status among our peers—the list goes on and on. We pursue prestige. We seek more and more money. We court local renown, or perhaps even broader fame. We amass nice things. One of the great modern ailments of humanity is enslavement to illusory pursuits.

If we get the prize, it strangely fails to satisfy as promised. If we fail in our quest, we feel unnecessary despondency. We're oddly depressed about not getting what would not have satisfied us if we had managed to snag it. And then, all too often, we just begin a new and equally illusory pursuit.

No man's fortune can be an end worthy of his being.

Francis Bacon

The meaning of life is not to be found in having lots of money, fame, prestige, or stuff. It's to be found in living your proper quest of positive achievement. Make a difference in the lives of other people, make a difference for good, create new relationships, new feelings, new structures of goodness in the world by what you do and who you are, and you will feel in that process what we so often seek with such futility in all the wrong places. The right sort of quest can be enjoyed at the deepest possible levels.

CONTEXT AND ENJOYMENT

When your work has meaning, it can be enjoyed in two different ways. Some things are *intrinsically* enjoyable—pleasant in and of themselves. A nice lunch, a great conversation, a new discovery can feel good apart from any consideration of their overall contexts. But when placed in the right context, things you're doing can become *extrinsically* enjoyable as well. Sipping a cool drink while watching a beautiful sunset can be an intrinsically enjoyable experience. The same thing relished in the context of an anniversary celebration with someone you love takes on a broader meaning, and more levels of enjoyment, that go beyond the immediate sense experiences involved. Seeing your work within the overarching perspective of a positive adventure, viewing it through the lens of creative growth and lasting good, will allow you to savor it on a much deeper level than is otherwise possible.

Contextualization can make good things better, and can even make difficult things good. This is an important aspect of the art of enjoyment. The Stoic philosophers made the important further observation that proper contextualization has the power to make even very bad things tolerable. And this in turn can help us to enjoy the goods we do have in our lives, in even the most difficult of times, while also helping us to have the energy and spirit to make things better.

All things are less dreadful than they seem.
William Wordsworth (1770–1850)

Contextualization is sometimes a tricky matter. The immediate context of something can occasionally make it look much worse than it is. My first weeks of living in my new hometown provided me with an interesting lesson in this. I was driving downtown for the first time, looking for the convention center. I was in my recently purchased dream car, a sporty convertible that I dearly loved but was as yet unaccustomed to driving. The street signs were confusing me as I drove along searching for my destination, and I suddenly realized I had missed my turn. As I quickly looked for a place to whip the car around, I spotted an available driveway on my left coming up fast. Without checking oncoming traffic sufficiently, I jerked the wheel counterclockwise and instantly saw that I was pulling straight into an oncoming car. I slammed on the brakes, but too late, and crashed right into the front side of a much larger vehicle, bringing both of us to a jarring halt.

What had just happened? The front bumper of my new car had plowed into another vehicle. Then contextualization clues started coming to my attention. There was an older man and a young boy in the car I hit. I looked up at the building next to us, and a large sign said "Police Department." A dozen people were on the sidewalk right beside us. They had seen the whole thing. Suddenly, I realized they were all wearing police uniforms. Funny how such things can come to our attention sequentially. One of these bystanders-in-blue ran around the car I had front-ended and peered into the driver's side. I'll never forget hearing him shout, in a voice of concern, "Are you all right, Mr. Mayor?"

Life is a series of surprises.
Ralph Waldo Emerson

Taking stock, the full, immediately available contextualization of this unplanned event was making things look, initially, pretty bad. A new resident in town, I had just rammed my new car into the mayor and his son in front of the police station, in full view of a large group of policemen equipped with pens and ticket pads, not to mention the equally visible guns and handcuffs. It looked grim.

But things are not always what they seem. The mayor and his son were unhurt. My bumper was barely scratched. The mayor's car was badly dented, but it was an old car and he told me he was ready to get rid of it anyway. I had stepped out of my car apologizing profusely and saying how embarrassed I was to be making the mayor's acquaintance in this way. Within minutes, we were talking about local events and my time at Notre Dame and the mayor was asking me about my work as a public philosopher. The crowd in blue dispersed as we talked, and I didn't get a ticket at all. The mayor left with a laminated wallet card on The 7 Cs of Success, and I returned home to my first free issue of a beautiful glossy local magazine that he edited. He had given me a year's subscription—as a welcome-to-town gift. To top it all off, when I walked through the backdoor at home, I was able to start my story by saying to my wife, "Guess who I just ran into?"

I think it a very happy accident.
Miguel de Cervantes

The ultimate contextualization of that little event ended up involving nice people undergoing an unfortunate but accidental occurrence, emerging physically unscathed, and all making the most of the moment to show some small kindness to each other. We put it into perspective, and our attitudes allowed us to go away having actually enjoyed some aspect of that otherwise bad experience. It was certainly the most I've ever enjoyed an automobile accident. I hope not to have that form of enjoyment too often in my life, but I'm glad that, on one occasion, I was able to experience such a small but vivid instance of people rising above an unpleasant situation, and in the process transforming it into a more positive episode.

Let's be totally honest about the challenges we occasionally have to face. Life sometimes contains a surprising share of unforeseen difficulties, avoidable and unavoidable pain, unexpected suffering, and even tragedy. This is a cosmic fact that unfortunately is not within our power to change. We do, however, have the power to decrease the overall suffering in our world, however extensively or slightly. And we should. But we can't do anything to prevent it completely. And we can't personally avoid an experience of it. It is, though, to an amazing extent up to us how we respond to the toughest challenges we inevitably face.

If you are distressed by anything external,
the pain is not due to the thing itself but to your own estimate of it;
and this you have the power to revoke at any moment.
Marcus Aurelius

Some of our emotional responses to events seem to be inherited from our family backgrounds, or picked up and reinforced by the patterns of behavior we observe from people we happen to be around. Ultimately, however, the attitudes we adopt and the emotions we cultivate all come down to a matter of inner decision and inner will. We can choose defeat or victory in our own spirits, a negative or positive take on what we've experienced, regardless of the course of external events.

This is a point made with great power by the psychologist Viktor Frankl in his book *Man's Search for Meaning.* While discussing what it was like to be a prisoner in a Nazi concentration camp, Frankl refers to "the last of the human freedoms—to choose one's attitude in any given set of circumstances, to choose one's own way." In even the worst of situations, it is possible to rise above the immediacy of suffering, and find a meaningful perspective for our lives that will allow us to refocus and endure, while appreciating the good that can always be found in a bigger picture of existence.

Some people seem to have a natural talent for transcendence. They can rise above anything, and it can appear almost effortless. But not all of us are equally gifted in this way. For many people, adopting a positive attitude in negative circumstances is a very difficult challenge. I've found that positive contextualization and positive attitude formation often seem to be easiest for people who have an overarching religious faith that puts everything into an ultimately benevolent cosmic perspective. But to say that it's easiest for people of faith may be misleading. Some devoutly religious people admit that taking up a joyous attitude in difficult circumstances, or even maintaining an even-tempered composure when things are bad, isn't at all easy for them. It's very tough. But it's precisely their faith that makes it possible at all. They sincerely report that, without the assurances of faith, they know they could not possibly confront certain difficulties with anything remotely resembling equanimity or inner peace. They see faith as necessary for dealing well with the troubles life sometimes throws their way. And they equally feel it enhances any good they experience as well.

I'm not talking about a vague spirituality that alchemically transforms negative vibes into positive feelings regardless of the harsh realities with which we have to deal. I'm referring rather to a deeply held set of beliefs about the nature of ultimate reality, a firm conviction that there is more to existence than meets the eye, and a connected confidence that we all live, work, love, and struggle within the ultimately redeeming intentions of a loving Creator.

The care of God for us is a great thing,
if a man believe it at heart:
it plucks the burden of sorrow from him.
Euripides

The faith that underlies and facilitates emotional transcendence most powerfully goes beyond intellectual beliefs and attitudinal commitments. It involves a felt direct connection and personal submission to something greater than the self. It involves a belief in, and a personal reliance on, a loving, forgiving, and yet morally insistent Creator God. A cosmic humility in the metaphysical arms of a divine benevolence and a firm hope that one day good will prevail seem to be the most potent ingredients for a resilient psychological transcendence of hardship. To put it simply and traditionally, individuals who feel they are living under the call and care of a provident God are typically the people most likely to have inner resources for rising above any calamity and hardship they might face along the way.

Theism, the traditional belief in a creative intelligence and benevolent spirit underlying the existence of the entire universe, can provide the ultimate positive contextualization for whatever happens to us in this world. It can be the foundation for the deepest possible enjoyment of life that is available to human beings. It can have a powerfully transformative value when it is properly lodged within a person's soul.

Whenever I have found my own journey going awry, whenever I have caught myself doing stupid, wrong things, having inappropriate reactions, and harboring self-defeating attitudes, it has been because this deep connection and contextualization of faith has faded from the forefront of my consciousness. I say this because I am a person who as a professional philosopher once spent many years and thousands of pages laying out and considering the intellectual underpinnings of theism, as well as of personal spirituality and religious faith. Yet even with that strong scholarly focus, I have had to learn the hard way that faith must be renewed daily in a deeply personal manner, or else its guidance is lost in our ongoing choices.

We are punished by our sins, not for them.
Elbert Hubbard

Whenever I have found myself in very unpleasant circumstances that were to any extent of my own making, it has always been in large part because of a failure of faith, a breakdown of that deep connection in the heart. And whenever I've found myself responding badly to challenges that were not of my own making, the root problem has been the same. The ancient conception of this separation from divine guidance, inspiration, and constraint has been that of a state of sin. Whether we use ancient concepts or modern ones, any alienation from what is deepest in life is a disconnection that will have a negative impact on any experience of life.

True ecstasy hails neither from the spirit nor from nature,
but from the union of these two.
Martin Buber (1878–1965)

I won't rehearse here the intellectual reasons I've discovered for being a theist or having faith. I've laid out all the main lines of thinking that I find both appealing and persuasive in three books already: *Making Sense of It All, God and the Philosophers,* and, most recently, *Philosophy for Dummies.* But I mention here the existence of such intellectual support to indicate that religious faith is not just a coping mechanism, endorsed only because and in so far as it can be of emotional and attitudinal benefit. It is best held because it seems, on examination, to be true. I bring this up here in at least a suggestive way because of its current power for good in my life, and in the lives of a great many people I know and respect. It can indeed provide the ultimate contextualization, the best guidance, and the deepest source of joy in any adventure.

I wouldn't for a moment want to imply that people without a religious faith can't practice the art of enjoyment in such a way as to facilitate and enhance their personal success in the world. They surely can. It's just that a certain form of contextualization, and thus extrinsic enjoyment, is unavailable within the confines of an agnostic or atheistic worldview. And that bears mentioning. In addition, many people who have made the transition from one worldview to another have claimed that a certain ineffable joy, a deep intrinsic form of enjoyment, is available only within the most transcendent perspective on life. And that is worth noting as well.

SIDE EFFECTS

When we're doing work that's right for who we are, or when we're living, overall, in a way that's deeply appropriate for our inner spirit, we can experience contentment, fulfillment, and a deep satisfaction in what we're doing. In order to understand how this is so, let's draw a few distinctions that are important to grasp.

Contentment is just a form of acceptance of the present as being what it is. This is altogether compatible with wanting the future to be very different, but is a state of inner emotional harmony which does not allow our progress forward to be impeded by such negative emotions as regret, resentment, and anger at perceived disappointments and injustices. Fulfillment is just the progressive realization of our potential. A sense of fulfillment is an awareness that our talents are being unearthed and put to a positive use as we grow into the people we are capable of being. Deep satisfaction is the coming together of contentment and fulfillment. It allows for the most thoroughgoing enjoyment of work and life.

The adventure of life is not a search for hidden treasure. The adventure is the treasure, if we live it right. If we treasure the process properly, we free ourselves from illusory quests.

Be it jewel or toy,
Not the prize gives the joy,
But the striving to win the prize.
Edward George Earle Bulwer-Lytton (1803–1873)

Here's the secret. The best way to enjoy your life is to have something to focus on other than enjoyment. And something bigger to focus on than just your life. Cultivate enjoyment, look for pleasure in what you do, adopt a spirit of playfulness in as many ways as you can, but always have in your life an overall structure of goals that are worthy in themselves to pursue, goals other than pleasure or enjoyment, toward which you can work. And always have goals that go beyond the confines of your own immediate self-interest. Only that can bring the deepest enjoyments. And only that will ultimately serve you best.

Let your delight and refreshment be
to pass from one service to the community to another,
with God ever in mind.
Marcus Aurelius

The times I have enjoyed the most in my life so far have been the magical moments that I was absorbed in play with my children, the hours or minutes engaged in fun communion with my wife, and those long stretches of time when I've been utterly immersed in creative work that is uniquely mine, work that's geared toward service to others. It's news to many people that work can rank right up there beside, or at least not far behind, the times you have with the people you love most. But it shouldn't be such a big surprise. We are created to be creators. We are meant to be joyous workers in the world. That's why achievement is so fulfilling and wondrous when it's right.

The labor itself is a delight.
Martial (ca. 40–ca. 104)

A sense of joy, a feeling of happiness, a state of contentment, is deepest and most lasting when it's the side effect of this process of true success, a form of personal work that moves in the direction of creating greater good for the world, in however small a way.

Labor is often the father of pleasure.
Voltaire

We need to understand better the concept of a side effect. One of the most frequently repeated mistakes in human life is to pursue as a focal goal what ought to be viewed as a side effect or by-product. A business that wants high customer satisfaction has to pursue other focal goals having to do with product quality and service excellence. Then customer satisfaction results as a great side effect. Parents who want their children to listen to them should set it as their focal goal to listen more to their children. The desired result then will be a side effect of a better relationship overall.

At their best, money, fame, power, and status are side effects of work well done in the pursuit of noble goals. So is the highest form of enjoyment. So is happiness. But in addition to being a wonderful side effect of the right sort of process, enjoyment can be the result of a deliberate art that moves the process along more reliably to its intended results. Our lives ought to be lived in pursuit of those noble goals that are right for our talents and dearest to our hearts. Then, the risks we take will most likely yield the results we value.

That is the deepest practice of the art of achievement. And that is where The 7 Cs of Success can take us all.

ACKNOWLEDGMENTS

I want to thank all the groups who have invited me to try out these ideas with them, and all those who have enthusiastically joined in their development through the years. You're artists of achievement who would make the great thinkers proud.

As always, I thank my family for their wonderful support and encouragement. They make it fun to be a philosopher each day.

I also want to express my appreciation to my agent, Reid Boates, for hanging in there with me on this one, the only one of my books that I've written and rewritten repeatedly over a period of many years as I've learned more deeply about success from not only the philosophers of the past but also the great achievers of the present day.

I hope that you, the reader, find these ideas applicable to your own adventure in life. If you have any stories or insights you'd like to share with me on any of these arts of achievement, I'd love to hear from you. Come visit me at www.MorrisInstitute.com, and e-mail me anytime. If my thoughts help you in your adventure of achievement, I'd like to know, so I can celebrate your success.

ABOUT THE AUTHOR

Tom Morris has become one of the most active business speakers in America due to his unusual ability to bring the greatest wisdom of the past into the challenges we face now. A native of North Carolina, Tom is a graduate of UNC (Chapel Hill) and has been honored, along with Michael Jordan, as a recipient of their "Distinguished Young Alumnus Award." He holds a Ph.D. in both philosophy and religious studies from Yale University and for fifteen years served as a professor of philosophy at the University of Notre Dame, where he quickly became its most popular teacher, in many years having as much as an eighth of the entire student body in his classes. He is now chairman of the Morris Institute for Human Values in Wilmington, North Carolina.

Tom's twelfth book, *True Success: A New Philosophy of Excellence,* lauched him into a new adventure as a public philosopher and adviser to the corporate world. His audiences have included General Motors, Ford Motor Company, Merrill Lynch, Verizon, IBM, the U.S. Air Force, International Paper, Price Waterhouse, Arthur Andersen, Target Stores, the Dayton Hudson Corporation, NBC Sports, *Business Week* magazine, Bayer, Deloitte and Touche, Federated Investors, Taco Bell, Minute Maid, the American Heart Association, and many of the largest national and international trade associations. He is also the author of the highly acclaimed book *If Aristotle Ran General Motors: The New Soul of Business* and the more recent *Philosophy for Dummies.*

Known by his Notre Dame students as "TV Morris," Tom is the first philosopher in history to appear in network TV commercials, where he has served as the national spokesman for Winnie the Pooh and Disney Home Videos, as well as being the only thinker ever to engage in early morning philosophy with Regis and Kathie Lee. He has also appeared on CNBC's early morning show *Business Today,* as well as on NBC's *Today* show with Matt Lauer. Tom is known for bringing the insights of the great thinkers into the drama of everyday life with high energy and good humor. His message is helping to change lives and revolutionize business practices everywhere.

THE MORRIS INSTITUTE FOR HUMAN VALUES

Built on the philosophical work of Tom Morris and his ongoing efforts to bring a re-energized vision of philosophy into the lives of as many people as possible, the Morris Institute for Human Values draws on the work of other living philosophers as well as the greatest thinkers of all centuries and cultures. It exists to encourage people everywhere to become more philosophical about their lives and wiser in their choices.

The mission of the Institute is to bring the wisdom of the ages into modern life in a way that matters. For this purpose, we have assembled a dynamic group of contemporary philosophers and organizational specialists whose ideas are helping businesses of all kinds around the world tap into their deepest resources.

We are providers of practical wisdom for the business of life.

Morris Institute Wisdom Retreats and Corporate Education Programs offer two ways of bringing the best practical philosophy into your life or into your company. If you've heard Tom Morris speak or read one of his books, you may have wondered how you could ground yourself more deeply in these ideas or spread them throughout your organization. Both our Wisdom Retreats and our Corporate Education Programs can be customized to give you, your associates, or your clients a more complete experience of this powerful philosophical approach to business and life.

Tom Morris and the Fellows of the Morris Institute will provide you with penetrating new perspectives on success, partnership, ethical leadership, and the nature of sustainable excellence in either of these forums. Come to the beach for a philosophical getaway or bring some of the most energetic contemporary thinkers into your place of business for a transformative experience. To find out more, visit www.MorrisInstitute.com and say hello.

06|21|23